D0730725

before
the last
all clear

*"The witty, yet deeply poingnant
memories of a man stil haunted
by the cruelties he endured"*

Daily Mail

Ray Evans

before the last all clear

By

Ray Evans

ISBN-13: 978-1492989684 Paperback
ISBN-10: 1492989681 Paperback

Cover Design | Layout | Formatting
by WP-WebWorks.com

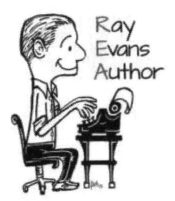

Children Learn What They Live

By Dorothy Law Nolte

If children live with criticism,
  They learn to condemn.

If children live with hostility,
  They learn to fight.

If children live with ridicule,
  They learn to be shy.

If children live with shame,
  They learn to feel guilty.

If children live with encouragement,
  They learn confidence.

If children live with tolerance,
  They learn to be patient.

If children live with praise,
  They learn to appreciate.

If children live with acceptance,
  They learn to love.

If children live with approval,
  They learn to like themselves.

If children live with honesty,
  They learn truthfulness.

If children live with security,
  They learn to have faith in themselves and others.

If children live with friendliness,
  They learn the world is a nice place in which to live.

Copyright © 1972/1975 by Dorothy Law Nolte

What Others Are Saying ...

Before The Last All Clear is a truly remarkable story. A boy, separated from his family and everyone he knows, deposited into the homes of those who would mistreat him, sets an inspiring example of strength and bravery. Rather than giving up, letting others drag him into an overwhelming swamp of stagnant depression, this boy stood fast against the demons that would strangle the heart of even most adults.

We here in the US rarely consider the last Great War from the perspective of a child, hiding as the bombs fall throughout the night, which is described perfectly, as though coming straight from a child's lips, not an adult pretending to think like one. This was a refreshingly raw and honest story, where little recognized battles fought by the children of the war were sometimes every bit as devastating. It's a story every American should read, so that we can understand how valuable our innocent childhoods of relative safety and security have been, and how lucky we are to never have fought a war on our own soil in recent history. It should be a part of classroom reading. And it should also be presented on film.

Thanks for sharing your childhood with us. It was very touching, especially the final reunion with Mrs. Williams, which brought tears to my eyes."

~ Ben Snyder, Beltsville, MD

"I have always found that the most compelling stories of our history are those of the people involved in it. This book, an auto biographical account of the story of a young English evacuee during the Second World War, had me hooked at the first words for that reason. I've always wondered what it was like for the people of Britain during those horrible days, and herein is an answer to that question. History is important not just because of the events, but because of the effect those events have on the human experience. This book is important for that reason.

You may find yourself, as I did, rejoicing, commiserating, sympathizing and despising all within a matter of a few pages. My guess though, is that you will be pleased that you read it. I got the feeling while reading, in fact that I was listening to my grandfather tell stories about the "Great War". Just the simple story of a boy put in an extremely difficult situation, trying to survive while far away from home, terribly lonely and afraid. But if you'd like to read a story about a boy who somehow makes due and even thrives in nearly impossible conditions, a story that is so obviously true that it hurts all the more to read, this might could quite possibly be that rare book that touches your heart."

~ Jerry Tietjens – Virginia, USA

"This book was a very, very moving story about a young boy who suffered miserably during World War II. It is magnificently written. Once you begin reading it is very difficult to put it down. You find yourself in this little boys' shoes of terror and a horrible life of starvation, beatings, and the lack of his true mothers love. I suggest anyone who can get their hands on this book should read it. Hats off to you Ray Evans."

~ Mary Huckabone – Virginia, USA

"I wanted to tell you I thoroughly enjoyed your book. I found your writing style easy reading, especially the parts that at the time must have been horrifying, but when relayed to the adult reader, are incredibly funny. The pool in the church is one. I just couldn't stop laughing. I could just imagine you with eyes wide open wondering what in the world they were doing. Your experience with the cigarette another funny story.

Your humor, intermingled with a true horror story, brings to mind the saying 'that which does not kill us makes us stronger.' It's actually very motivational and shows your inner strength prevailed and kept you going. Your stay with Mrs. Jones was difficult, but with the Simmons, well how you were treated is incomprehensible. It makes me wonder just how many children didn't make it back home, how many didn't survive the separation from their families and poor treatment by the surrogates?"

~ Cheryl Sciecinski

"I found the book fascinating, heartbreaking, and intensely moving. The thoughts and feelings of the common man about the war are seldom told in history books and the perspective of a child is never heard. This book takes you into the world of a child whose universe has been shattered. Everything he knew, even the people he loved were taken from him. It is a story filled with love, fear, confusion and triumph. Mr. Evans tells his story simply and honestly. I found the book impossible to put down—I was in that time with him, living through what he lived through.

I highly recommend this book."

~ Lynnda Petersen

"Ray takes us back to those days and tells us what it was like, the desperations, the fear, the need to make life changing decision on a moment's notice, even the hunger and the cold. He also shows us himself in those days, a child of amazing strength, separated from his family, moved from one unhappy 'billet' to another. In his writing, he has been able to convey the extraordinary hard- ships he endured but he does not seek our pity."

~ Felicity Vaughan Swayze

"While reading, I found myself fighting with Ray to survive, cheering his minor victories, and admonishing those who caused him pain...all the while thinking could I have the strength to walk in his shoes? The straightforward, 'plain-talk' style of the author made this a book I not only couldn't, but didn't want to put down.

Thank you, Ray, for sharing your story."

~ Adrienna Smith

"I read this entire book in one sitting. I read many, many books and this is definitely one of my favorites. I will definitely read it again. It is a wonderful and powerful story. There is no better way to learn about people than to hear or read their story. Ray was very generous to share his story with the world."

~ Derek York

"I literally felt like I was there and while my heart broke as the adult world looked at the big picture and often times didn't see this little boy, this is a story about a child who knew it was all going to be up to him now. This book is not a tragedy it is a gift of love to anyone who reads it. Every adult who he has a child needs to read this book. This is the only book I have bought in hardcover and I will buy the sequel. I cannot wait to see what happens."

~ Alexi K. Hilton

"I wasn't sure what to expect when I first picked up this book. To my surprise, I was instantly taken back to WWII and found it difficult to put the book down.I must say, Raymond handled himself much better than I would have, especially with Mrs. Simmons. The book gives you a chance to experience real events during WWII, but also gives you a glimpse into humanity and how each person handles the situation in front of them. I would highly recommend this book to anyone and thank you Mr. Evans for putting your memories onto paper so that I could re-live this time with you."

~ Pamela Kosmowski

"I have just finished reading your fabulous book. From the start was easy to recognize your very unique style of storytelling, you write just like someone talking. I "became" that little 6 year old boy and enjoyed it from cover to cover—and you were right! It made me cry, several times, but it also made me laugh right out loud many times. I was sad to come to the last page and look forward to your next book."

~ Jeanette Davis

"I too was an evacuee during the war. *Before the Last All Clear* brought back so many memories as I began reading. Please let me know when the sequel is available so that I may purchase a copy."

~ Kenneth J. Beech

"I have just returned from England and I saved your book for the trip. I really enjoyed it, and it was hard to put down because I wanted to see what happened to you."

~ Jill Musico

"I read your book in less than two days, a feat that I haven't done in 40 years. Be sure to let us know when your next book is available."

~ Russ Fill

Acknowledgments

I'm deeply indebted to my daughter Debbie. Had it not been for her, these stories of my wartime evacuation would still be locked away in the attic of my mind. "They need to be put down in writing," she told me, "so that they can be passed on to your grandchildren." Never in my wildest dreams did I think they would be published one day.

My sincere thanks and appreciation go to my sisters, Elsie and Muriel, and to my brothers, Frank and Stan, for allowing me to continually badger them for their memories.

To my Welsh mother, Mrs. Williams, and her family for their incredible kindness and influence they had on my life during the two and a half years I lived with them. Thank you, I'll be forever grateful to you.

My undying appreciation to the many thousands of foster parents who readily came forward and took us evacuees into their homes and accepted us as part of their families.

To my son Ray, who lives in England. We love and miss you.

And above all, I dedicate this book to my dear wife Lilian for her support and profound patience during the eight years it took me to write it ... I love you.

Table of Contents:

* * * * *

Before The Last All Clear

By

Ray Evans

1939

This Morning the British Ambassador in Berlin handed the German government a final note stating that unless we heard from them by eleven o'clock that they were prepared at once to with- draw their troops from Poland, a state of war would exist between us. I have to tell you now that no such undertaking has been received, and that consequently this country is at war with Germany."

~ Neville Chamberlain, Prime Minister

War Is Declared

As the summer began to fade in 1939, events took place that would change my life forever; I would never be the same again.

It didn't matter where you were in England, whether you were in a shop, a pub, or in the street, the general conversation in 1939 was about war. It was even impossible to listen to any of the programs on the wireless without it being constantly interrupted by the latest bulletins. Then the moment the wireless was turned off, the nightly discussions would commence between my father and uncles as to the likelihood of war. "Ah it's just rumors, that's all it is," one would say. And then someone else would chip in, "It'll all be over by Christmas, you mark my words"—the exact words that were spoken by many people just before the First World War started. From my bed late into the night I could hear them talking in the kitchen, trying to convince each other that it was "all propaganda and nothing else."

The rumors originated from the preparations the authorities had been surreptitiously putting in place for many months before the outbreak of war. Most important of all, of course, was the *evacuation scheme*. Great Britain, being an island, obviously relied heavily on the weapons, munitions, raw materials, and foodstuffs that flowed to her ports from countries like the United States, Canada, and other places around the world. The Germans knew that if they could paralyze Britain's ports, including Liverpool, London, Southampton, Swansea, and many others, consequently cutting off their supplies, it would give them an excellent chance of starving Britain into submission.

As early as 1938, long before Mr. Chamberlain's announcement of war, because of the German's threat to use poison gas, an adequate supply of gas masks, close to 40 million, had already been issued to adults and children all across Britain. Within a few months of war being declared, brick constructed air raid shelters suddenly started to appear on all the streets. In some cases, if there wasn't enough room on your street for an air raid shelter, council workmen or volunteers were sent along to erect one in your garden. Free to those who earned less than five pounds a week, these weren't made of brick, but were simply erected by digging an eight foot by four foot hole at the bottom of your garden and lining it with corrugated metal sheets. They were called Anderson shelters, named after their inventor Sir John Anderson, the Lord Privy Seal at the time. The ones I remember were just large enough for four bunk beds, two on each side; whether they erected any larger ones in personal gardens, I'm not sure.

The Home Guard was formed in May 1940 by Sir Anthony Eden, then Secretary of State for War. Liverpool, my hometown, was one of the major ports in those days (the gateway to the

Atlantic as it was often termed), and because of that, the government was certain that it would be an early target for the German *Luftwaffe*. They were later proven right when the British and

American intelligence captured the German naval archives after the war and it was stated in the minutes that Liverpool was in fact to be the "Number One Target."

In just those first few days of September 1939, approximately 3 million children were evacuated to safe areas all over Britain, even to places as far away as Canada and the United States. An amazing logistical accomplishment by the authorities in such a short time, by anyone's reckoning. In the autumn of 1940, with the onset of the Battle of Britain, a second evacuation of approximately 1.25 million women and children took place. For many evacuees it was a new adventure and the start of a love affair with their new country that most would never forget. In fact, there were some evacuees who were given more love than their own parents gave them. But for others, including myself (except for the last two years when I stayed with the Williamses), it would be a traumatic experience that would stay with us forever. While, on occasions, I was to suffer mental abuse by the families of the household, it didn't stop there. For the first couple of years, until my Liverpool accent faded into a Welsh accent, I was continually taunted in school for being an evacuee, and told in no uncertain terms to get back to Liverpool where I came from. Up until 1943, when I moved in with Mrs. Williams, if it had been possible, I would have walked back to Liverpool anytime—bombs or no bombs.

Over the years, many evacuees have returned to relive the happy memories they remember of those bygone days and to show their children the place where they were given a warm and sympathetic welcome, something the Welsh people are widely known for, and, of course, a safe refuge from the bombs.

Altogether, I lived in six different homes. Later, I'll tell you why I ran away from three of them.

Considering we were still feeling the effects of the depression, life in Liverpool for our family before the war was no different than most working class families. The worst hit areas for unemployment were in the northern areas of Britain; one in four men was out of work (Ruth Ingles. 1989. *The Children's War*. William Collins Sons & Co. Ltd). My father, George Ernest Evans, wasn't a professional man; his living was mainly earned by doing the various laboring jobs he was lucky enough to find. Sometimes a job would last only a few weeks before he was back on the road again looking for something else. And it was always the same old story wherever he went ... "Sorry, no jobs today, try again tomorrow." But Dad never gave up—he made sure he was on that factory doorstep the next morning before anyone else. And if he wasn't lucky there, he'd jump back on his bike and cycle to the next factory, and the next one after that, quite often arriving home long after everyone (except for Mam) had gone to bed. Because he couldn't afford to go in a café for something to eat, she always had a hot meal waiting in the oven for him when he got home. Things got so bad that even the factories that weren't laying off workers were eventually forced to shut down.

One of his many jobs was cleaning windows, but he didn't keep it for long. The money wasn't very good, and it nearly cost him his life. When he was cleaning the windows of a pub on Belmont Road, someone inside accidentally pulled the window down on his fingers. They hadn't seen him because they didn't bother opening the curtains. For a few agonizing seconds, until he managed to get his footing on the ladder again, the hand that was trapped was the only thing that prevented him from falling three stories down.

Those were the days before the Welfare State, when poor people received little help from the government. Anyone who applied for assistance (Mam and Dad didn't) would feel stigmatized should friends or neighbors find out. Those who asked for financial help were subjected to the Means Test, a visit by inspectors from the local authority for interrogation as to their means, subsequently making them feel like beggars. An inventory of all their household possessions would be taken, and once completed, the cold-hearted inspectors would suggest they sell items of furniture, such as a couple of chairs, to pay their rent. It didn't matter that those poor souls had nothing to sit on, if it meant using boxes for chairs, then so be it. People were well aware that if they couldn't pay their rent, the entire family would be evicted and sent to those Dickensian establishments known as work- houses, the places that we read about in *Oliver Twist*. The good old days were not so good for the unemployed.

Beatrice Marion, my mother and a woman who possessed a fearsome courage in facing life's difficulties, was twenty, and George, my father, was twenty-two when they married in 1923. Although it would be another three years before they started a family, by 1939 Mam had given birth to no fewer than nine children, five boys and four girls, in descending order, George, Elsie, Frank, Muriel, Albert, Raymond (that's me), Stanley, Dorothy, and Edith.

I was born approximately two hours before midnight on the twenty-ninth day of August, 1933. The First World War had ended eighteen years earlier, and the great depression was already four years old. 1933 was the year *King Kong* made its debut,

"Stormy Weather" was the top song, and, above all, an evil-minded man called Adolph Hitler became chancellor of Germany, later to become the *Fuehrer*. The Second World War was still six years away.

So, with the help of the local midwife, at around ten in the evening, my life began in the front parlor of Number 11, Holinbourn Place, a suburb of Norris Green, which at that time was on the outskirts of Liverpool.

My father would tell his children how much farther up the social ladder my mother was when they met and how his future mother-in-law at first disagreed with the union, saying that her daughter was marrying beneath her. Yet together my mother and father made a family that was respected by everyone, including her mother and the rest of the "well-off" Poingdestres.

Mam was the typical caring mother and loving wife. Her job was to look after the home and children and, under very difficult circumstances, make ends meet. There was no electricity in those days, no refrigerators, no washing machines, no vacuum cleaners. The clothes had to be boiled in tubs and scrubbed on washing boards. Then, after they'd dried on the line outside, the creases were taken out with an iron-shaped piece of metal that was heated on the fire. And because there were no carpets, floors had to be scrubbed on hands and knees. "A woman's work is never done," was one of the many sayings my mother often quoted—she was certainly right about that one.

Great emphasis was put on good manners, and the family was brought up with those Victorian values and standards that were maintained by discipline. My Dad? Well, he always had the ability to laugh at himself, which taught his children humility, while my mother taught us manners and courtesy. He would lecture us at length that any goal could be achieved by using common sense. He would say success was ninety percent common sense and not to forget to use it. Do not undersell yourself or allow others to climb over you. When I think about it now and consider that my father was the sole breadwinner of the family and the country was still in the grips of the depression, I can't remember any of us having to go hungry or being without fire in the grate. Years later I remember him telling me that the job he hated most was working on the fishing trawlers. It was extremely hard work he told me, but because the pay was so good he managed to stick it out until he joined the Royal Air Force. Twice a week he was allowed, free of charge, six fish to take home. That might not seem very important now, but with so many mouths to feed it was an enormous help. The problem was that the fish were so big the only way he could carry them was to hang them from the inside of his oilskin coat, making it very awkward to ride his bike. Consequently, even though he was exhausted at the end of the day, he was forced to walk the three-mile journey home. He was a good man and a good father. Except for the cost of a packet of Woodbines, every penny of his wages was given up to Mam for housekeeping.

At the beginning of 1939, things really started to look up. Dad's job on the trawlers was bringing in good money, which in turn enabled us to move to a nicer house in a nicer district. It was a newer, more modern house in the rural, tree-lined district of Tuebrook, just beyond the city limits.

Mam fell in love with the house even before she stepped inside. The only major concern she had about the house after her and Dad had finished looking around was whether they could comfortably afford the higher weekly rent of eight shillings and sixpence. "I'd love to live here," Mam said, "but eight shillings and sixpence is a big jump from the seven shillings we're paying at the moment." "I think it's worth it," Dad said. "It's more modern than the house we're in; it's got three good-sized bedrooms, and it's got an indoor bathroom and toilet." The luxury of an indoor bathroom and toilet did the trick, and we moved in a week later.

Because of the distance between our new house and our old one (about two miles) and the fact that Dad couldn't afford to hire a furniture removal company, the only other alternative was to move our things with the aid of a handcart. So on that Friday evening on his way home from work, he cycled to Breck Road where he arranged to pick one up the following Saturday morning. He had to sign an agreement stating that if he was fifteen minutes late in returning the cart, the hire charge would be doubled from a shilling to two shillings.

I don't know how many journeys it took Dad and George (my eldest brother) to complete the removal on that Saturday, but I know it was far too many for them to even stop for a quick cup of tea. As it turned out, it was just as well they didn't because they returned the cart with just minutes to spare.

While everyone was busy carrying furniture and boxes inside the house, and because I wanted to be the first to explore the miracle of indoor plumbing in our new house, I sneaked upstairs to the toilet. And there, I have to admit, was where I reveled in the luxury of being the first one in our family to pee into the white majesty of the brand new toilet bowl. After pulling the chain, I spent a few more minutes in the bathroom sitting on the side of the bath, gazing at and running my fingers over the beautiful smooth enamel and wondering at the thrill of not having to bathe in a metal tub anymore. For the first time in my life I found myself actually looking forward to bath night.

We all loved our new house on Brookbridge Road, with its modern kitchen and brightly distempered walls and ceilings. It was much nicer than our other house on August Road, everything was so new and clean. There was even a little patch of soil under the front window where Mam planted a couple of rose trees. I can't begin to tell you how happy we all were there. At this particular time, of course, it was inconceivable to even imagine what was about to happen to us all the following September.

＊ ＊ ＊ ＊ ＊

It's Monday, the fourth of September 1939. The time, about 8:30 in the morning. We've just left the house to go to school—George, Elsie, Frank, Muriel, Albert, and I. We always leave at the same time because Elsie likes to spend a few minutes in the school playground before the morning bell sounds, and also because she

hates being late. Personally, I couldn't care less if I ever went to school. I hate it. I tell Mam every single morning, just like I did today before we left the house, that I really do hate going to school. But it doesn't make any difference—she still makes me go. She keeps telling me that she can't under- stand why I hate it so much when I've only been going a short while. She says, "You better get used to it young fella-me-lad, you're only six for God's sake, you've got another ten years to go yet before you can leave."

I think the reason I'm feeling much worse than normal about going to school today is because the summer holidays have suddenly come to an abrupt end. That was a terrible shock, finding out I've got to go back to school again. But of course what I do not know, and neither does anyone else, is that when we do arrive at the school, things are going to be quite different than any other normal day. We don't know that in little less than half an hour, we'll suddenly find ourselves, along with everyone else in the school, being sent home again. And not because the headmaster has suddenly decided to give us an extra holiday, far from it, we'll all be sent home today so we can prepare for an evacuation.

As we file into the assembly hall for the usual prayers and hymn singing, everyone thinks it strange to be ushered to their seats without even being handed a hymn and prayer book. We are soon to find out why. A few minutes later when everyone is seated, the headmaster comes onto the stage holding a piece of paper in his hand. He stops when he gets to the middle of the stage, holds the piece of paper high above his head, and brings immediate silence by stamping his foot hard onto the stage floor. When he's got everyone's attention, he reads it aloud:

> "Today, each and every one of you will be given a letter
> to be taken to your parents inviting them to a meeting which
> will be held tomorrow morning at nine o'clock in this
> assembly hall. The meeting is to discuss the evacuation of all
> children away from Liverpool to a safer place. This will be for
> the duration of the war, therefore, there will be no more
> school until further notice."

There's a shocked silence when the headmaster finishes reading the letter, but it only lasts a few seconds, then panic breaks out. The headmaster has to stamp his foot down on the stage again and tell everyone to go back to their seats and to file out properly like they normally do.

Because I was only six at the time and too young to comprehend the seriousness of the situation, the closing of the school was music to my ears. I couldn't understand what all the panic was about. We've just come back from six weeks of summer holiday, and now we were going to get another holiday.

When we arrive at the house, Elsie dashes into the kitchen where Mam is sitting glued to the wireless listening to the news. She's been there ever since we left for school this morning, listening to all the bad news. "Mam! Mam! The headmaster's told us there's going to be a war and we've all got to be evacuated." Mam quickly switches the wireless and tries to calm Elsie down. She's just as frightened as Elsie but tries her best not to show it. She tells Elsie the evacuation is just a precaution and nothing more.

> "We'll probably be sent to North Wales for a few weeks, that's all."

> "But why would anyone want to kill us?" Elsie asks.

"We've done nothing to them."

"No one is going to kill anyone," Mam says. "It's just a load of rumors, that's all."

Although he never said anything that day, George wasn't convinced at all. In fact, he spent half that night getting in and out of bed looking through the window to see if he could see any German planes in the sky.

At the school meeting the next day, in addition to a letter containing all the arrangements for the evacuation, the parents were given a list of items that the children had to take on their journey.

<u>BOYS</u>

1 overcoat or mackintosh

2 vests

1 set of pyjamas

2 shirts

1 tie

2 pairs of pants

1 pullover

1 jersey

1 cap

1 pair of boots, 2 if possible

2 handkerchiefs

1 comb

1 towel, 2 if possible

1 bar of soap

1 toothbrush

1 gas mask (must be carried at all times)

Also enough food should be brought for
the day of travelling, e.g., sandwiches, biscuits,
and apple and an orange.

GIRLS

1 coat or mackintosh

2 dresses

2 vests

2 pairs of knickers

2 sweaters

2 pair socks (white)

1 nightdress

1 bar of soap

1 toothbrush

1 hat

1 pair of shoes, 2 if possible

1 gas mask (Must be carried at all times)

Also enough food should be brought for
the day of travelling, e.g., sandwiches, biscuits,
and apple and an orange.

In the evening, after our meal, Mam and Dad carefully go over the list they've been given at the school. Mam's out of her mind because there's so much to do in so little time. "What's going to happen to our furniture and things?" she says to Dad. "We can't leave it here." "We'll split everything between your parents and mine," Dad says. "I'm sure they won't mind looking after it all until we come back after the war. Anyway, don't worry about that now, I'll sort it all out when everyone's left."

Then, on top of everything else, Mam suddenly realizes we all need new shoes to travel in, but the trouble is there's no spare money to purchase even one pair of shoes, never mind six pairs. Dad's beside himself at this dilemma—he cannot bear the shame he and his children might feel. I have to get the money from somewhere, he says to himself, but where? Long after everyone has gone to bed he sits in the armchair by the fire trying to think of a solution. Finally he comes up with the answer … the gas meter.

Like so many houses in those days, our house on Brookbridge Road was illuminated by gaslight. The gas supply entered the house by way of a coin-operated meter. At the side of the meter was a little metal box that stored the pennies. Being a large family, by the time the Meter Man came around every three months to empty it, our meter box was so full Mam sometimes had difficulty trying to get another coin into it. After unlocking the padlock from the meter door, he would scoop all the pennies into a bag, carry it upstairs into the kitchen, and then empty it out on the table. To make it easier for him to count the money, he'd meticulously put all the pennies into little stacks of twelve, then line up the stacks in groups of twenty. (Twelve pennies equaled a shilling, and twenty shillings equaled a pound—this was all before decimalization, of course.) Consequently, when he'd finished, there were five groups of twenty stacks lined up across the table, making a grand total of five pounds. To give some idea of what five pounds was worth then, Dad would have to put in at least sixty hours in just one week to earn anywhere near that.

I don't know if all the Meter Men counted the money this way, but that's how our collector man did and it took him ages. Once he was satisfied the total amount agreed with the meter reading, you were given a portion of the money back, a discount they called it. Just like everyone else in those days, Mam was always glad when the meter man was due.

One of the problems with having a gas meter back then was that it was a big temptation for burglars, especially in the older houses where the meter could be seen through the fanlight above the front door. The burglar always knew which houses had a meter and which ones didn't. The break-ins got so bad at one point that it wasn't uncommon for a burglar to break into several houses in the same street on the same night. "Bloody Gas Meter Bandits were at it again last night," you could hear people say. All he had to do was enter the house from the rear, take a chair from the kitchen to reach the meter, snip the padlock off the cashbox, and help himself to the money. When you came downstairs the next morning and saw a chair sitting under the fanlight, you knew right away you were one of the unlucky ones.

In desperation that night Dad crept down the stairs into the basement, broke the lock off the meter box and stole all the money. It wasn't until many years later, when I asked Elsie about it, that I would discover the truth about where my father had found the money to buy us all new shoes. Learning the truth of what had happened helped me to understand the statement my father quoted to Elsie: "Needs must when the devil drives."

In order to leave this sinister crime unsolved, a few days after my mother and the three younger ones had left for South Wales, Dad volunteered for the Royal Air Force. After a short spell in Liverpool, he was posted to the RAF camp at Pembrey, which, luckily for us, was only a short distance from Llanelli, the town we were all evacuated to. My father's basic education as a boy was sparse to say the least, and yet, during his first two years in the RAF he studied hard and became a Medic. As the war progressed he was posted to a military hospital in the Middle East for the remaining two and a half years of the war. By studying equally as hard, he eventually passed his exams to become a State Registered Nurse.

Anyway, as I've mentioned, part of the money he took from the meter went toward buying us all a pair of canvas shoes, which in those days were called plimsolls (leather shoes were too expensive). The remainder Mam used to purchase four or five Hessian sacks to make haversacks for us to carry our things in. There were no suitcases in our house; we didn't travel anywhere to need one.

Time was short so Mam stayed up all that night so she could have all the haversacks ready for the next day. The worst part, she said, and what took the longest, was undoing all the sacks before she could start making them up. She even made time to sew one for George's friend John Griffiths who lived across the street. Griff (his nickname) was known and liked by all our family. Elsie didn't know it at the time, but ten years later she would marry John and have a daughter to him. They were happily married for over fifty years, until his death in 1998.

On the eve of the evacuation, while Elsie and George helped my mother with the packing, I laid awake thinking about my very first train journey. Except for Mam and Dad, none of us had ever been out of Liverpool before, never mind on a train—I was so excited I could hardly wait for the next morning to arrive.

George (13) and Elsie (11) were shocked to learn that the authorities had told Mam in the meeting that all mothers with children under school age (Stanley, Dorothy, and Edith) would have to follow at a later stage. So my two eldest siblings listened attentively to my mother's instructions as to how to take care of us younger ones during the long journey to South Wales. She knew she could depend on them—her and Dad had brought us up that way.

The headmaster had given strict instructions to the parents at the school meeting not to be late on the morning of evacuation. He'd stressed that all children who were to be evacuated must be assembled in the schoolyard, ready to go to the station, no later than 8 a.m.

It was common for soldiers to be arriving on the same trains that children would then be bundled onto to take them to the countryside.

Operation Pied Piper

–

Pandemonium & Precious

Goodbyes

It's a quarter to seven already, fifteen minutes since Mam came into our bedroom to wake us all up. George and Albert are already downstairs eating their breakfasts, and here I am, awake long before those other two opened their eyes, still laying here waiting to get up. I wish Mam would come up and wake our Frankie instead of shouting from the bottom of the stairs. He keeps poking his head out of the sheets and shouting,

"OK Mam. I'm up. I'm up."

If I could sleep where he sleeps, on the outside of the bed instead of against the wall, I wouldn't have to lay here every morning waiting for him to wake up so I can get out of bed. I've been tempted to get up and climb over him, but I'm too scared. I did try one morning, but I lost my balance tripping over our Stanley, who sleeps in the middle, and fell on top of Frankie. Our Frankie's always grumpy in the mornings on the best of days, but that morning, when I fell on top of him, he just went crazy. He chased me around the room like someone who'd lost his mind. "I'll break every last bone in your body if I catch you, you stupid little sod," he kept saying. It was a good job Mam heard the rumpus and came up and saved me.

Mam has made us all a bowl of porridge for our breakfast, something she usually only makes in the winter. She says, "I know it's still summer, but you all need something solid in your stomachs for the long journey." After we've finished breakfast, we get our coats on and line up to say goodbye to Dad. He can't come to the station because he has the job of looking after Stanley, Dorothy, and Edith until Mam gets back.

To give us plenty of time to get to the school for a quarter to eight, we leave the house just after seven o'clock. When we get outside in the street, we join the long procession of mothers and children making their way to the school. Mam quickly shepherds us into the middle of road so we can tag onto the end. After walk-ing a couple of hundred yards, and it being a calm and sultry morning, we have to take our coats off again.

When we get to the school there are already lots of children lined up waiting to begin the three-mile trek to Lime Street Station. We're taken into the main hall, the place where we usually have our morning assemblies. They've taken all the chairs away so they can put trestle tables out for people to sit behind, with clipboards and pencils. When we line up in front of them, they write our names and addresses on luggage labels and tie them to our coats. Then we move onto the next table where they look inside our haversacks to make sure we've got everything with us, such as our ration book, identity card, clothing, and sandwiches. And after they've done that, because of Hitler's promise to gas us all if we don't surrender, they check the cardboard boxes that we're carrying over our shoulders to make sure our gas masks are inside and that they are working properly. And then they tell us, just like the people on the last table told us, that we must always carry our gas masks at all times, no matter where we are, even when we go to the toilet.

I look at Albert with my hand over my mouth trying not to laugh. I can't help thinking what it would be like to be sitting on the toilet with a gasmask on.

Even though I'm leaving my mother behind, I feel safe with Elsie. She's like a second mother to me. Eleven years of age, that's all my big sister was then, but she was old far beyond her years, there was no doubt about that. When she wasn't in school, instead of playing out with her friends, she would help Mam in the house. Quite often, when Mam was getting Dad's tea ready, she would wash us little ones and put us to bed. Mam even taught her to darn our socks and mend our clothes. "A stitch in time saves nine," Elsie was always saying, just like she'd invented the saying.

Mam's eldest daughter always had a matronly power over us all, even after we left school and we were working for a living. It's hard to imagine what Mam would have done without Elsie, especially in those times. I must say though, my big sister could be very strict when she needed to; she wouldn't think twice of giving you a clip over the ear if you were naughty. We all used to call her bossy boots under our breath. When she'd tuck us into our beds, she'd say, "I don't want to hear a sound from any of you, do you hear?" Then, just as she was about to go out of the bedroom, she'd pop her head around the door and shout, "BREEEATHE and you'll be in trouble, do you hear me?

Just BREEEATHE."

Outside in the schoolyard, the teacher that's escorting us to the station lines us up in twos and tells us to hold hands—Elsie holds mine. We move off when the teacher blows her whistle. As we make our way through the streets with Mam and all the other mothers behind us, people come out of their houses to wave and shout goodbye. I ask Elsie why some of them are crying but she doesn't answer.

> Gasmasks, haversacks, and pillow cases
>
> Plimsolls instead of shoes.
>
> We're marching to Lime Street Station,
>
> Holding hands in columns of twos.

There are thousands of people in Lime Street, all pushing and shoving trying to get into the station. Mam says that it's pandemonium, and that she's never seen anything like it before. Half the population of Liverpool must be here she says. It's even worse inside the station. There's an army of children screaming and crying all over the place, teachers struggling to tear them away from their mothers, trying to get them on the train. People are walking over clothes, shoes, and food that have fallen out of pillowcases and bags that the younger ones are struggling to carry. We're all glad Mam made us these haversacks.

We finally get to our carriage just in time to hear the station porter shout the all aboard. Mam's eyes fill up with tears as she quickly holds each of us in her arms. I've never seen Mam cry before. She tells us to be brave and look after each other on the journey. As George steps onto the train, Mam takes a sixpence out of her purse and puts it in his pocket, telling him it's to buy us each a penny cup of cocoa at one of the stations.

When the train pulls out of the station, we all crowd around the window to wave. We keep waving and waving until we can't see her anymore. Elsie is crying so much she shakes all over. George puts his arm around her and says,

"Don't worry Else— we'll be OK."

Mams and Dads on the Platform,

Waving their sad goodbyes.

The train snakes out of the station,

Tears in everyone's eyes.

With the exception of my father, the entire family was evacuated to South Wales. At first it wasn't possible for everyone to stay together, so except for the three youngest ones, Stanley Dorothy, and Edith, the rest of us were split up during the six years from 1939 to 1945.

Evacuee Distribution Center

The Human Cattle Market

It was an old steam train that slowly rattled its way to its destination, stopping at practically every station to pick up more evacuees, and occasionally for water. By the time we board, all the seats in the compartments had been taken, so we stand in the corridor the entire journey. The train is very crowded, making it difficult to move around. I don't mind at first, as I have a good view of the countryside through the window. I was so taken up seeing the sheep and cows and horses in the fields, I think I stood there for at least half the journey. It was all new to me; I'd never seen the countryside before. But once darkness fell and I couldn't see anything, I asked Elsie if we could get off the train and go back home. Throughout the journey lots of children were crying or sick. I often wondered how Elsie and George coped with us all on that long, twelve-hour journey to South Wales. A journey I'm sure none of us will ever forget.

We stretch out on the corridor floor to try and get some sleep but it's no use as people keep tripping over us trying to squeeze past. Someone asks one boy who's trying to get past where he's going. He says he's going to the toilet. There aren't any toilets on the train they tell him, you have to wait until the next station to use the toilets there. He says he can't wait and gets up on the seat and tries to pee out of the window, but it all blows back on him.

The train eventually makes its way across the Welsh border into the town of Llanelli, "the land of the Joneses and the Williamses." It blows its whistle as it enters the station, slows down, and comes to a halt alongside the platform. It's about 11 p.m. and Liverpool seems a million miles away. We're very tired and hungry, and not in a very cooperative state. The novelty of my first train journey wore off many hours ago. We all spill out onto the station platform where we are lined up for a head count. I can hear people shouting in some foreign language, but I can't see them properly because of the steam that's whirling everywhere. Then someone behind us shouts, "I hope we're not in bloody Germany."

After the teacher finishes the count, George puts his hand up and asks for permission to go back on the train to get Frank's gas mask. The teacher comes over to Frank and tells him off. "Your gas mask must be carried at all times," she says. "Do you understand?" Frank's afraid to look up, so he just nods his head and says yes. "And don't you ever forget it," the teacher says. "Do you hear me?" He nods his head again and says, "Yes, miss. I'm sorry." Elsie feels sorry for Frank and puts a protective arm around him. She tells the teacher that the reason her brother has left his gas mask on the train is because neither him nor any of us are accustomed to carrying gasmasks around with us. The teacher comes over to Elsie and says, "There's a war going on young lady, it's for his own good." Elsie says, "Yes, miss. I'm sorry. I understand."

We march out into the street, leaving the station deserted and quiet again. The locals, all volunteers, are waiting to transport us to a school hall a couple of miles away. They've been there for hours, some in cars, some in vans, some in buses. When we arrive at the school we see a big sign on the hall door: *Evacuee Distribution Centre.*

The Evacuee Distribution Center is the place where our "borrowed parents" are waiting to make their choices, a moment in time, I have to say, which will be stamped on our minds forever.

As we enter the hall, we are each given a brown paper bag. Inside are two cheese sandwiches and a few biscuits. For a beverage, we have a choice of a cup of tea or a glass of lemonade. The allocation of children to their foster parents is like a cattle market, that's the only way I can describe it, and it's a terrible day for us all. Some of the evacuees are from the poorer areas of Liverpool, and because of their scruffy appearance, give a preconceived notion that we are all lacking in good manners and discipline. It's just as well Mam isn't here today, seeing all these people considering and mulling over the selection of a child.

The time has finally come for us all to be separated. A sickly feeling wells up inside Elsie's stomach as she listens to people all around her saying, "I'll have that one," or "I'll take this one." "I don't want that one, I want a boy." She tries to calm herself and remember the instructions Mam had given her and George on who was to stay with whom—Albert with George, and me with her and Muriel. These instructions had to be obeyed to the letter, they had not been given lightly. Elsie knows that if Mam had known the rule that any foster parent taking more than one child could not do so unless they were of the same sex, she would have advised her accordingly. So no matter what anyone says today, she's determined to carry out Mam's instructions, no matter what.

The man from the Red Cross comes over to where we're all sitting and asks Elsie why I have a bandage on my head. She tells him I tripped and cut my forehead a couple of days ago. He bends down to get a closer look.

"Did they put stitches in the cut?"

"Yes," Elsie says. "Three."

"It's bleeding slightly," he says, "which means one of the stitches may have come out. Come with me Raymond."

Elsie panics and pulls me back. "You can't take him, he's got to stay with me."

"I'm just taking him to the Red Cross to have his wound examined," the man says. "Don't worry, I'll bring him straight back."

After he's put two new stitches in my head and given me a new bandage, he brings me back into the hall. Elsie is at a table talking to the billeting officer and an elderly lady. When she sees me, she comes over and takes me to one side. I can tell by her face that something is wrong.

"I've been trying to get them to put you and me together," she says. "Just like Mam told me to do, but they say they can't do that. They say the rules state that boys have to go with boys, and girls have to go with girls. There's nothing I can do about it, I've been trying all the time you were away getting your new bandage on. They've split all of us up differently, George with Albert,

Muriel with me, and you with Frankie."

I look over at the lady she's been talking to.

"You're not staying with that lady," Elsie says. "She's mine and Muriel's new landlady. The lady that you and Frankie will be staying with hasn't been able to get here; there's a man waiting outside in his car to take you to her house."

Mrs. Davis, our billeting officer, says that it's getting very late and that we must leave right away. She says the volunteers that are waiting outside to transport us to our billets are getting impatient because they've been up since early morning. She says we should have been out of the hall over an hour ago. Elsie apologizes to Mrs. Davis for keeping everyone waiting. "I know you were trying to do the right thing for everyone, Mrs. Davis says, "but we do have to abide by the rules."

The three volunteers have their engines revving, they're impatient to leave. We all say goodbye to each other and race to the cars out in the rain. Our very first ride in a car would have been a novelty we would have enjoyed considerably more had it been under different circumstances. But Frank and I just sit in silence as we are driven through the dark, empty streets to our new home and new mother.

* * * * *

Elsie and Muriel's billet is a little white house on the top of a very steep hill. Mrs. White, a tall, elegant, silver-haired lady opens the door and leads them in. She takes them through to the lounge to meet her husband and Dawn, their sixteen-year-old daughter. Dawn would normally be in bed by this time, but her mother has allowed her to stay up so she can meet her two new "stepsisters" (a name she tells her mother she prefers to call them). After a cup of tea and a rock cake each, Elsie and Muriel are taken upstairs to be shown their bedroom. "This is Dawn's bedroom normally," Mrs. White says, "but because there are two of you now and not just one as first arranged, Dawn has agreed to move into the little box room instead." That makes Elsie feel rather guilty, knowing she was the one who finally talked Mrs. White into taking in two evacuees instead of one like she'd originally intended. "I'm sorry," Elsie says. "I feel terrible Dawn has to move out of her nice bedroom just because of us." "Don't worry about that," Mrs. White says. "Dawn is very excited to have you here as a matter of fact; she's always wanted a sister, ever since she was little."

Mr. White has worked for the railway ever since he left school at fourteen. He's a train driver now, been one for the last ten years as a matter of fact. And just a few days ago his boss called him into the office and asked him if he'd like to take over the Devon Route. "It will mean working a couple of nights on occasion," his boss told him. "But I didn't think you would mind that, considering you come from that area." Mr. White didn't need any time to think it over. In fact, he was so excited at this offer that he couldn't pedal home fast enough to give the good news to his wife. At first his wife wondered why he was so excited about being given a new route, especially having to start working nights again.

"You hate working nights," she tells him.
"I know," he says, "but think about it. My brother lives in Devon, and he has a farm there."
"I know that," she says, "but I still don't know what you're getting at."
"Extra food," he says. "That's what I'm getting at."

"Yes, of course," she says. "I didn't think."

"And you've volunteered to take in an evacuee when they arrive. Don't forget that's another mouth to feed."

"What do you think your brother will let us have?"

"Well, where there's a farm there are chickens, and where there are chickens there are nice fresh eggs."

Mrs. White's eyes light up. What with the rationing starting, she knows all too well she'll be lucky to get any eggs, never mind fresh ones. "We'll be able to have fresh eggs for breakfast every morning," she says to her husband.

"Yes, and not only that," he says, "we'll be able to have as much bacon, meat, and vegetables as we want."

Because the tremendous shortage of food during the war resulted in a very extensive black market, Mr. White's brother told him that he must be very careful no one finds out about their little scheme, otherwise they could both land up in jail.

On their way out to school each morning, Mrs. White would give Elsie and Muriel an apple from the sack her husband had brought back from Devon. The odd occasion when they were allowed to help themselves, Muriel took an opportune moment to sneak a couple of extras. She always felt guilty doing that, but she loved apples so much she couldn't resist the temptation. She'd hide them under her armpits until she got outside, then, when the coast was clear, she'd take them out and give Elsie one. Elsie, as always, strongly disapproved, and she would tell Muriel that she was brought up better than that, but she still ate hers.

They were very happy living with the Whites and they stayed there for three years until Elsie, at fourteen, was old enough to leave school and get a job. She and Muriel moved onto the same street as Mam lived on, just three or four doors away. George was already living with my mother and had a job working in the tin works. Elsie's first job was working as a waitress in an Italian restaurant, from 9 a.m. until 9 p.m. Her weekly wage was seven shillings and sixpence, about $3 in today's money. She stayed there for about a year until she found a better paying job working in the tin works with George. The extra five shillings in her pay packet was an enormous help for my mother, but the job was by no means an easy one. It entailed lifting very heavy sheets of tin and weighing them, and because of the unbearable heat from the furnaces, she could hardly find the energy to walk home. Elsie, thinking she could raise her weekly pay by as much as a shilling a week, the amount my mother agreed she could keep to boost her pocket money, decided to leave the tin works after a few months and took a job in the steel works. The hours were no different, the day shift was 9 a.m. to 9 p.m., and the night shift was 9 p.m. to 9 a.m. At the time, both these factories in Llanelli were the main industries providing materials for the war effort.

Sometimes on my way home from school, I'd sneak into the factory where Elsie worked to ask for a penny to buy a comic or some sweets. She wore a big leather apron, and two pieces of leather tied to her hands to protect her from the sharp edges on the metal sheets. Besides the unbearable noise in that factory, the heat was so intense from the furnaces that it was very difficult to breathe properly. It certainly wasn't woman's work, that's for sure, but because of the extreme shortage of manpower, the factories had no choice but to employ women instead.

* * * * *

Through a mix up, Frank and I were put in the wrong billet that night. "I wanted two girls," the lady kept telling the man who delivered us there, "not two boys. I've got two girls of my own. I don't want boys mixing with my girls." Frank and I stood on the lady's step, in the pouring rain, wondering what was going on. But after a very long discussion with the lady, he managed to talk her into taking us in until an alternative billet could be found. "There's so many we have to find new homes for," he told the lady. "But I do promise you, I'll get the billeting officer right on it as soon as possible."

I don't know why, but for some reason the billeting officer was not told of our whereabouts, and consequently we were immediately put on the "lost list." For two weeks Mam, Elsie, Muriel, and the billeting officer must have searched the whole town, until one day someone spotted us playing outside the house. The billeting officer didn't waste any time that day, and we were swiftly taken to our proper billet, the one we were allocated in the first place.

An Artic Welcome

Where's The Door Knob?

O ur new billet is a three bedroom, terraced type, not far from the city center, about five miles from Mam's billet. There are only about fifteen houses on each side of the street; ours is number seven at the bottom end, where the chip shop and pub are. At the other end of the street, the cobbler shop is on one corner and on the other corner is the church.

The welcome we get when we arrive isn't anything like Frank and I expect. Mrs. Jones, our new landlady, is outside, busy polishing the brass knocker on her front door. She's a short, plump lady with straight graying hair tied in a tight bun on the back of her head. Mrs. Davis, our billeting officer, has to tap on her shoulder to get her attention. Mrs. Jones stops what she's doing and turns around to face us. Mrs. Davis puts her hand out to shake hands. Mrs. Jones, not bothering to even speak or look at Mrs. Davis, ignores her outstretched hand and stares straight at

Frank and I. The expression on her face terrifies me. When she's finished looking us up and down with her cold, steely eyes, she turns her back on us and carries on polishing, polishing the brass knocker she's been polishing for the last thirty or more years. "Take them round the back," she says. "They can't come in this way."

Mrs. Davis, shocked at this lady's behavior, taps her on the shoulder and says, "Excuse me, but would you mind telling me how I'm supposed to know which house it is round the back?" Mrs. Jones cups her hand around her ear, and in her razor-sharp tongue says, "WHAT? What did you say? Can't hear very well."

"HOW WILL I KNOW WHICH HOUSE?" Mrs. Davis repeats loudly.

"Its number seven," comes the impatient answer. "Just go down to the bottom of the street, turn right into the lane that leads to the back of the houses, and walk up the lane until you see a green gate with a number seven on it, that's the house."

On the way around, Mrs. Davis knows by the look on our faces that Frank and I are certainly not looking forward to staying with Mrs. Jones. In fact, from that moment on I had an instant dislike for Mrs. Jones that stayed with me until the day I left.

"Don't worry," Mrs. Davis says, trying her best to console us. "We must have caught her at a bad time. She wasn't like that when I came to see her the other day."

When we arrive at the gate, her husband is already waiting for us at the scullery door. "This way," he shouts, waving his hand. "This is the house." Mrs. Davis leads the way along the garden path. "I'm scared," I whisper to Frank. "I don't want to live in this house. Ask Mrs. Davis to take us somewhere else." "I will," he says. "Don't worry, I will."

Mr. Jones shakes hands with Mrs. Davis and then with Frank and me. It's a strong, powerful handshake, which makes my fingers turn white. I like Mr. Jones straight away. "Come in and take your coats off," he says looking really pleased to see us. "I've put the kettle on for a cup of tea." We all sit down in the kitchen. "Sorry she sent you round the back," he says with a smile on his face. "She's a moody old bugger sometimes. Even I'm not allowed to come through the front door, and I pay the bloody rent. All she does all day is cleaning, cleaning, and more bloody cleaning, she'll rub the house away one day. But don't you worry about her, her bark's worse than her bite." Mr. Jones who looks to me like he's in his late seventies, stands about five feet ten inches tall, and has a full head of yellowy gray hair.

The billeting officer, who does not have any desire to speak with our new landlady anymore, gulps her tea down, thanks Mr. Jones for taking us in, and quickly beats a retreat out through the scullery door as fast as she can.

Mr. Jones suffers with severe attacks of asthma, sometimes every day, caused by spending all his working life down the local coal mine. Frank and I take a liking to the old man straight away. He's a kind, gentle person, who goes out of his way to make his two evacuees from Liverpool more than welcome. His wife, on the other hand, is a very domineering woman who never ceases trying to train her husband to march to her command. Since his retirement, and because of his wife's obsession with cleaning and polishing every hour of every day, he spends most of his days sitting alone in his cane rocking chair in front of the kitchen fire, either listening to the wireless or reading the newspapers.

When our landlady finishes polishing the brass outside, she comes into the kitchen and tells us to follow her upstairs. "This will be your bedroom," she says. "It's where my two sons slept before they went off and got married. You must keep it clean and tidy like they always did." She's very proud of her two sons. The eldest is a doctor in a Swansea hospital, and the other is a practicing lawyer with a successful company in the same city. I'll tell you about them later.

She stands over us to make sure we fold our clothes properly before putting them into the dressing table drawers. When we've emptied our haversacks, she points to a sheet of paper that's lying on the dressing table. She passes it to Frank and says, "These are the rules. I want you to read them carefully and if either of you refuses to abide by these rules, you'll have to find somewhere else to live. Do you understand?" We both nod. "When you've finished reading the list, come down and I'll show you the rest of the house." We sit on the bed while Frank reads the rules aloud:

✓ No relatives or friends to be invited into the house at any time.

✓ Take shoes off at the kitchen door.

✓ Do not enter the house by the front door.

✓ Upstairs bathroom is out of bounds. Use the sink in the scullery.

✓ The parlor and dining rooms are out of bounds.

✓ The pantry is out of bounds.

✓ Every morning, empty and clean chamber pot.

✓ Make the bed before you come down to breakfast.

✓ Breakfast: 8 a.m. sharp.

✓ Evening meal: 4:30 p.m.

✓ Bedtime: 8 p.m., except on Saturdays: 9 p.m.

After he finishes reading the list, we have a quick look around the bedroom before going downstairs. Besides a dressing table, it has a big, high bed and two very big wardrobes. The wardrobes are so big they nearly touch the ceiling. Back home the only bedroom in our house that had a dressing table was Mam's bedroom. We're overwhelmed with such grandeur.

She shows us the rest of the house by starting at the parlor, a room reserved for special occasions; ordinary visitors are taken to the kitchen. She points her finger at the door. "This is the parlor," she says. "It's strictly out of bounds. You would have seen that on the rules sheet." She then pulls a key out of her pocket, waves it in front of our faces, and says, "It's always locked and I'm the only one with the key." We walk further down the hall to another door. "This is the dining room," she says, "and again, there's no reason why you should have to come in here either. You'll eat your meals in the kitchen." We walk a bit farther until we reach the last door before the kitchen. "This is the pantry, which I've mentioned on your list. This also is under lock and key."

The house is much larger than it looks from the outside. All the rooms are at least twice the size that I expected them to be. We go into the kitchen. Mr. Jones is sitting by the fire listening to the wireless. At one end of the kitchen is a Welsh Dresser displaying a large collection of 'Willow Pattern' dishes. At the other, a highly polished cast-iron fireplace with a mantelpiece so high that it has to be cleaned with the aid of a stepladder. On the hob at the side of the fire is a big iron kettle, a kettle she once used for boiling water. It has a shiny brass lid and a shiny brass handle— another item on her extensive polishing list.

At exactly eight o'clock that evening she comes into the kitchen and tells us to go to bed. Bryn says to let us stay up and listen to the show on the wireless, but she says no. She says it doesn't finish until nine o'clock, and that's far too late for us getting to bed. "I've set the alarm clock for seven thirty in the morning," she says, "that way they can be down here by eight o'clock, washed and dressed."

Because the *Tommy Handley Show* is one of Frank's favourite shows, Frank tries to talk Mrs. Jones into letting him stay up to listen to it. He tells her Mam always let him stay up an hour longer on Thursday evenings so he could listen to the *Tommy Handley Show*. "I don't care what your mother let you do," she says. "You're in my house now, and you'll do as you're told."

When we get upstairs she follows us into our bedroom dragging a chair behind her. She places the chair under the light, then climbs up and takes the bulb from its socket. "You'll have to get undressed in the dark." she says. "I don't want the ARP Warden banging on my door in the middle of the night." (The Air Raid Precaution (ARP) Warden patrolled the streets during blackouts to ensure that no light was visible from the houses, so that the German bombers could not use the light source for targeting their bombs.)

When she closes the door, Frank fumbles his way over to the window to open the curtains, forgetting about the blackout. It's just as dark outside as it is inside. Then, as we're about to get undressed, the bedroom door opens just wide enough to allow Mrs. Jones to stick her arm around and take the doorknob off. "The old bitch has locked us in," Frank says. "She's taken the doorknob off so we can't get out. As soon as I see the billeting officer next I'm going to ask her to move us. I'm not staying here with her."

Half past seven the next morning the alarm goes off, we jump out of bed, get dressed as quickly as we can, and wait to be let out. When it gets to quarter to eight, she still hasn't come up, so Frank decides to bang on the door. "After all that lecturing last night," he says, "about us being dressed and washed by eight o'clock this morning, the stupid old bitch has forgotten to let us out." He bangs on the door for ages and ages until he gets fed up and sits on the bed again. Then, when he hears Bryn's voice coming from the hallway, he jumps up, bangs on the door, and shouts, "Mr. Jones, can you hear me? We're locked in the bedroom." Mr. Jones comes up and lets us out. He hadn't heard us knocking because he'd been in the garden talking to his next-door neighbor.

When we get downstairs Mr. Jones is telling his wife off for locking us in the bedroom. We wait behind the door for them to finish. "It's not my fault I couldn't hear them banging," she says. "You know what my hearing's like, you've been married to me long enough."

"They wouldn't have to bang on the door if you hadn't taken the doorknob away," Bryn says. "Why did you do that? Why did you lock them in their bedroom?"

"Because I don't know whether to trust them or not," she says. "How do I know how they've been brought up?"

"They are not like that," he says. "I told you that before they came here."

Mrs. Jones doesn't answer and goes into the scullery. She fills the bowl with water and tells us to come in and get washed. When Bryn comes into the scullery and sees us washing in cold water, he takes the kettle from the stove and warms the icy cold water with hot water. From now on, he says, they get washed in the bathroom, not down here.

Coal House Jackpot

It was a constant battle between Bryn and his wife in those first few weeks. But as time went on, he did manage to change most of her rulings toward us. Except for using the bathroom that is, she never did give in to that. "They can bathe in the metal tub on Friday nights when we're out," she told him. "That metal tub was good enough for us, so it's good enough for them."

Friday nights are the only nights they go out together. I don't know where it is, but it's always the same place, the same place they've been going to for the past forty years, Bryn says, and he still hates it. He says he doesn't like it because of the type of people that go there. "They're all a lot of hoity-toitys," he says. "A bloody crowd of snobs." Bryn says one fella that goes there won't even talk to him and they've known each other since they were kids. The same fella he says who was sent to school with holes in his shoes and the arse ripped out of his pants. "Who does he think he is for Christs sake? I hate going to that bloody place."

The other reason Bryn doesn't like going there is because of the way he has to get "dressed up" as he calls it. He'd rather go in his corduroy baggy trousers and flannel shirt, but his wife always insists that he wear his best Sunday suit and tweed cap when they go to these meetings. He doesn't mind that so much, having to wear his best suit and cap, it's the collar and tie he doesn't like wearing. He's never liked wearing a collar and tie. Not a single Friday goes by without them getting into an argument about that one.

"There's no law saying you have to wear a collar and bloody tie as well as a suit," he tells her. "Not all the men wear collar and ties."

"I've told you before," his wife says, "just like I tell you every week, what they decide to wear is no concern of mine."

"If it wasn't for this bloody collar stud," he tells her, "I wouldn't mind wearing a collar and tie."

Trying to get the stud through the little hole in the front of his collar is Bryn's worst nightmare. He's never accomplished it yet without dropping it on the floor at least a half dozen times.

* * * * *

The bathtub hangs from a big nail on the coal shed wall. It's hung in there so long that parts of it have gone rusty. It used to hang on the back of the scullery door, but that was before Mrs. Jones got her new bathroom installed. So as soon as they leave the house, Frank and I go down to the garden, carry the tub into the kitchen, sit it down in front of the fire, and start filling it withkettles of hot water. When it's half full, we top it up with cold water. When Frank's finished having his bath, we boil some more kettles of water to warm it up again for me.

One Friday night, just as I was about to step into the bath, Frank tells me to get dressed again and go and get a bucket of coal for the fire. He said he'd go for it himself if he hadn't already had his bath. But that was just an excuse, and I told him so. I told him he was sending me for the coal because he didn't want to go out in the pouring down rain. I told him the only times he goes for the coal is in the daytime or when it isn't raining. Anyway, it didn't make any difference what I said, I still had to get dressed and go for it.

I hated having to go in that coal shed at the best of times, but especially when it was dark and raining. And the rain on that particular night was so heavy, I was drenched to the skin before I even got anywhere near the coal shed. And that's not all. When I did get inside, the torch suddenly packed up on me. I shook and banged it a few times expecting it to come back on again, but all it did was to give a couple of faint flickers before packing up all together. I thought the only thing to do was to go back to the house and tell Frank about the torch not working, and that I'll get the coal tomorrow. And if he insists that I go back tonight for it, I'll stand my ground and tell him to go and get it himself. But then Mrs. Jones suddenly flashes across my mind. She's pointing her finger at Frank and me and saying, "Don't let that fire go out you two, or you'll be in serious trouble when I get back."

With that thought in mind, I crouched down and started groping around in the dark for the shovel. It was usually lying on top of the coal where the last person was supposed to leave it, but it wasn't there on this particular night, they'd put it somewhere else. I cursed whoever it was for not leaving the shovel in its usual place, because now I had no alternative but to start digging the coal with my bare hands.

It wouldn't have been so bad using my hands if Frank had agreed that I bring just large lumps, as they were easy to find in the dark. But he wanted some small lumps as well, and they were always deep down under the slack. And digging deep down under the slack was not something I was looking forward to. Not because my hands were numb with the cold, no it wasn't just that, it was because I didn't want to get stinking cat poop all over them like Frank did one time. I remember sitting in the kitchen with Bryn when he dashed into the scullery shouting, "That dirty bloody cat from next door has shit in the coal shed again and it's all over me." Bryn and I couldn't stop laughing. "Cat shit's supposed to be lucky Frank," Bryn said to him. "Maybe you're going to come into money." "It's not funny," Frank said. "If I catch it, I'll kill the dirty little sod."

Anyway, I finally got the bucket filled with a mixture of big lumps and small lumps, just as Frank had asked me to. What I didn't know, until I got back in the house that is, was while I was digging under the slack for the small lumps I unknowingly scooped up a coin. Frank saw it in the bucket when he was putting some coal on the fire.

"Hey look at this," he shouted. "Look what I've found! It's a three penny bit."

I jumped out of the bath to get a closer look. He was right, it really was a three penny bit.

He went into the scullery to wash it under the tap. When I was dressed I asked him for it back. "It is mine," I said, "It's me that really found it."

"I know you found it," he said, "but don't forget, I could have thrown it on the fire if I hadn't seen it in the bucket. So, I think it's fair that we split it, just like I did with you when I found that penny that time."

"I know you split the penny with me," I said, "but I never got any of it. You lost it in that slot machine."

"Look," he said, "as soon as we get to a shop tomorrow, I'll get it changed and give you your half. OK? Fair enough?"

I nodded, but I wasn't convinced. I had a pretty good idea what his real plan was.

The next morning, after we'd finished all our chores, we put our coats on and set out to the newsagent on the next street to get our money changed. Just as we were about to go in, Frank stops in the doorway.

"I was just thinking," he said, "instead of getting it changed in here, why don't we go to Station Road, get a milkshake, and change it there?"

"That's just an excuse," I said. "You don't want a milk-shake, you want to go in the milk bar so as you can play on the slot machine."

"So, what if I do? What if I do want to play on the slot machine? It's a free country."

"I don't care," I said. "I don't care what you do, just as long as you don't put my half of the money in it as well."

Frank had developed a keen fascination for that slot machine from the moment he first played it. I kept telling him on the way there that just because he'd won on it the first time, didn't mean that he'd win every time. I tried very hard that day to change his mind, but he wouldn't listen, he had his mind firmly set on playing the slot machine and there was nothing I could do to change it.

"There's nothing to worry about," he kept saying. "I know exactly how the machine works now. I watched some lad playing on it the other day. He kept on winning every time he put a penny in. and all he was doing was shaking the machine from side to side to make the ball go in the winning hole." And amazingly enough, by doing that, Frank won on his first three goes. I was ecstatic as I watched him scooping handfuls of pennies into his pocket. "I told you so," he said. "I told you I'd win."

Then, as Frank stretched up to put another penny in the slot, the owner of the milk bar came up behind him and grabbed him by his collar.

"What the hell do you think you're doing?" he said. "Shaking the bloody machine like that? I've a good mind to take that money off you and throw you both out in the street." The man's grip on Frank's collar was so tight, Frank could hardly talk properly.

"I'm sorry, sir," he said in a squeaky voice. "I didn't mean to shake it. I won't do it again."

"You better not," the man said, "otherwise you'll be out on your ear."

I expected Frank to put the penny back into his pocket, but he didn't. As soon as the man went away, he put it in the machine. This time the ball dropped into the little hole at the bottom, the little hole that said "Lost" on it. Frank looked over at me and shook his head. "I'll try one more time," he said. "If I lose, we'll go." As he took another penny out of his pocket he turned to see if he was being watched. The grimacing expression on the man's face was enough, so Frank just carefully pressed the penny in the machine, stood back with his hands in his pockets, and waited for the ball to come out of the hole at the top. Frank didn't take his eyes off it as he watched it bounce between the tiny metal pins. At first he thought it was going to drop in one of the winning cups, but it suddenly changed direction and dropped into one of the losing holes instead. But only by a fraction, all it needed was that little push and a shove and he would have won another thrupence. I wanted to ask him to stop playing before he lost everything, but I knew he wouldn't listen, so I sat in the corner and waited. I sat and waited until I saw the last penny go in the machine.

"You could have given me my half before you lost it," I said, as we made our way home. "I could have bought a pork pie from next door, I'm starving."

"Oh why don't you stop moaning," he said. "All you ever think about is your stomach."

Because the outside toilet doesn't have any electric lighting, and I'm frightened of the dark, I always (now that Mrs. Jones doesn't allow me take a torch with me anymore) try to measure my stomach calls.

"You only have yourself to blame," she said one day as she took the torch away from me. "You don't need to leave it switched on all the time you're in there, running the batteries down like you do. In the future you can take a candle with you, that's what we had to do when we were using it. I can't afford to be paying out for new batteries every other day just because you don't like sitting in the dark."

"But what about the wind," I asked. "It keeps blowing the candle out all the time."

"Then you've only got two choices haven't you?" she said. "You can either go to the toilet in the dark like your brother does, or (and she said this with a slight smirk on her face) you'll just have to go on nights when it's not windy."

I hated having to use that old lavatory, and it wasn't just because it didn't have any electric lighting—there were plenty of other problems with it as well. For one thing, the flushing mechanism didn't work anymore, which meant of course you had to take a bucket of water with you to flush it. And second, because the latch was missing off the door, the only way you could keep it closed (especially when you're sat on the toilet) was by holding onto a piece of string that was tied to a nail on the inside of the door. The string idea was Frank's, and it worked quite well as long as you kept tight hold of it. If you didn't keep tight hold of it, it would always swing open again, sometimes without you noticing it. And after what happened to Frank on one occasion, I personally (just to make sure) have always wrapped the string around my hand at least six times.

He was sat on the toilet one day so completely immersed in the comic he was reading, he hadn't noticed he'd unconsciously let the string fall out of his hand onto the floor. And it wasn't until a gust of wind suddenly blew up, that he realized what he'd done. He tried his best to reach for the string before the wind blew the door open, but unfortunately he was too late. Consequently he was left sitting there with his trousers around his ankles in a very embarrassing position. And what was even more embarrassing for Frank that day was that Marion, Mr. Cartwright's daughter from next door, happened to be in the garden at that precise moment. She said she'd never seen anything so funny in all her life. Watching Frank sitting there with his pants around his ankles and not being able to do a thing about it.

Frank and I sometimes use the toilet upstairs, but that's only when Mrs. Jones is out and Bryn gives us the key to get in. He has tried on many occasions to talk Mrs. Jones into letting us use their bathroom, but he's never succeeded, not up to now anyway. All it does every time is end up in a big row between them both. And that doesn't do Bryn any good, having rows all the time, it just makes his breathing even more difficult.

Rabbit Head For Dinner

Most of the rows were due to Bryn's excessive smoking. Of course, you couldn't blame her for nagging him about that, after all it was for his own good. A couple of ounces of thick-twist was no problem for Bryn to go through just in one single day. But sometimes, because of her insatiable desire for tidiness, she'd nag him unnecessarily over silly, unimportant things. Those were the times when Frank and I felt really sorry for him. For instance, she'd nag him over leaving his fingerprints on the brass rail that hung below the mantelpiece, or laying the poker down on her nice clean hearth instead of standing it up in the corner in its proper place. Silly as it may sound, that was one of her pet hates, the poker being put in its wrong place … unbelievable.

"She's right," he said to me one day after them rowing over his smoking. "I shouldn't smoke; it's bad for my chest. It's full of coal dust you see, Raymond. That's what working down a coal mine all your life does for you; feeds the family well but fills your lungs up with bloody coal dust. I have tried to stop smoking, many, many times, but after a few days I just start up again. And my breathing has got so bad now I can't even tend my garden anymore. I used to love my garden, you know. Each Sunday, as soon as I was back from church, I'd go upstairs, put on my overalls, and spend every daylight hour out there. I had the best vegetables around here, I don't mind telling you; you can ask anyone that." He pointed his finger at the window. "Look out there," he said, "and tell me what you see, and I don't mean the lavatory or the coal shed, what else do you see?"

I went over to the window that looked onto the back garden. "Do you mean the air raid shelter?" I said. "That's the only other thing I can see."

"That's right," he said. "An air raid shelter, and it's right in the middle of the bloody garden. I know we've got to have an air raid shelter, but look where they've put it, right where I grew all my vegetables. Now I can't grow any vegetables, now when we need them most because of the rationing. Why didn't they put it on the other side of the garden next to the coal shed? I wish I'd have been here at the time; they wouldn't have got away with that, the stupid buggers."

* * * * *

Meat was one of the many products that became very scarce once food rationing began, and on the odd occasion when it did show up in the butcher's window, it was so expensive most people couldn't afford it anyway. For that reason, rabbit became a very popular substitute. It was nothing in those days to see rows and rows of rabbits hanging on a rail outside a butcher's shop.

Fortunately for Mrs. Jones and some of the neighbors on our street, they didn't have to buy their rabbits from the local butchers; theirs came from old Mr. Cartwright next door. I say fortunately, because not only were they able to buy their rabbits from Mr. Cartwright at a far cheaper price than they could from the local butchers, but they didn't have to skin them either. Mr. Cartwright did that for them at no extra charge. He was out practically every day chasing rabbits, and he was good at it as well; he used to take me with him sometimes.

The first time Frank and I were given rabbit for our meal in the Jones household was on the second Sunday after our arrival. I remember that particular meal time like it was only yesterday, and you'll understand why when I tell you what she put down in front of us that day.

It was the day when Mrs. Jones's two sons and their wives were paying their fortnightly visit. Every other Sunday after attending morning service, they'd head straight to their mother's house to spend the rest of the day there. And because rabbit pie happens to be Edwin's favorite meal , it's always rabbit pie she makes for their dinner, and it never changes.

"You never bother asking their wives if they'd like something different," Bryn said to his wife one Sunday morning as she was preparing the meal. "I know I would like a change now and again, and I'm sure the others would."

"Edwin likes rabbit pie," she replied, "and until he wants something different, rabbit pie is what it's going to be, and that includes you and everyone else. I'm not running a restaurant here."

Edwin, the older of the two sons, is a doctor by profession. Clifford, her other son, works for a law firm. Mrs. Jones is very proud of her two sons, Edwin especially. Besides being the owner of a goodly sized bank account, Edwin also happens to be the proud owner of a recently purchased motorcar as well. And because of that, Mrs. Jones likes nothing better than to be standing at the front door as Edwin draws up to the house. From there, she has a fairly good view of all her neighbors who happen to be peeping through their curtains at that precise moment.

"You're just an out and out bloody snob," Bryn shouted up the lobby one day as she stood with the door open. "That's all you are, an out and out bloody snob."

"No, I'm not," she said. "I just like to be at the door when they come, that's all."

"And that's a load of cods-wollop as well," he said. "It's only recently you've decided to greet them at the front door. Before, when Edwin didn't have a car, they had to walk round the back like everyone else.

As soon as everyone has arrived and taken their coats off, they're led straight into the dining room to have their meal. As always, Mrs. Jones has timed the meal for exactly ten past one, ten minutes after their arrival. She knew she could rely on Edwin not to be late, and he never was, not even a minute late. Amazing when you think how far he had to come, all that way from Swansea. But Edwin knew all too well what his mother thought about people arriving late and messing her schedule up.

On this particular Sunday she told everyone not to wait for her and to start eating. She would join them as soon as she'd seen to Frank's and my meal. We were already sat at the kitchen table with our arms folded when she came through. She didn't like you resting your arms on the table, especially when you were eating. If she saw you doing that, she'd give your arm a quick slap with the back of her hand. "Its bad manners," she'd say. "The table is for eating off, not for slouching on."

The smell from the rabbit pie drifted into the kitchen as she lifted our meals out of the oven. I couldn't wait for mine.

She brought Frank's meal in first. When she put it down in front of him, Frank was so shocked and flabbergasted at what was on his plate that he jumped up from his chair, nearly knocking her over, pointed his finger at his plate and said, "That's a rabbit's head. I'm not eating that; I'm not eating a rabbit's head."

"Please yourself," she said, "if you don't want it, then don't eat it; you'll get nothing else." She went out and brought mine in and it was the same, another rabbit's head. It was sat right in the middle of the plate just like Frank's, surrounded by pie crust, potatoes, cabbage, and turnips. It made me feel sick just looking at it, especially at the holes where its eyes used to be.

After she'd gone out, Frank went out into the garden and dumped both of the rabbit heads into the bin. But he wouldn't pick them up with his hands; he slid a pencil through the eye sockets and carried them out that way.

As I sat eating the rest of the meal, I asked Frank whether he knew if Welsh people liked eating rabbits' heads.

"I don't know," he said, "but if they do, they're not going to make me eat them."

"Shall I go and tell her we don't like the rabbit's head Frank?" I said. "And that we only like the other parts."

"No," he said, "You know what she's like, she'll get annoyed. Just eat the other stuff on your plate if you're hungry."

"What about your potatoes and stuff Frank? Aren't you hungry?"

"I am, I'm starving, but you can have mine if you want it. I'm not touching anything; not after that thing has been near it."

That evening when they'd all gone home, Bryn, Frank, and I were sitting around the fire in the kitchen tucking into a baked potato that Bryn had baked in the fireside oven. Still inquisitive as to whether Welsh people really did eat that part of the rabbit, I asked Bryn if he did. He lowered his newspaper onto his lap and with a curious look on his face said,"Rabbit's head? Good God no. Why would I want to eat a rabbit's head?"

Frank gave me a sharp nudge to keep my mouth shut. "Oh nothing," I said, "I was just wondering, that's all."

"What's she been giving you?" he asked. "She didn't give you the rabbit's head for your dinner did she?"

"Please don't tell her, Mr. Jones," Frank said. "It doesn't matter now; we never ate it anyway. We threw it in the bin"

He jumped up from his chair, screwed his newspaper into a tight ball, and flung it across the kitchen. "I'll throw her in the bloody bin," he said, as he stomped his way along the hallway to the parlor. "Fancy giving anyone a rabbit's head to eat. I wouldn't even give one to a dying dog, never mind a human being."

Bryn and his wife had a terrible row over the rabbit's head business that night. So bad in fact that Frank and I got frightened and decided to make ourselves scarce and go to bed early. We didn't go to sleep for a while, wondering what she might do to us the next day.

"She'll be mad with us, Frank, won't she? I wonder what she'll do to us?"

"I don't know what she'll do, but whatever it is, it'll be your fault for opening your big mouth. You want to learn to keep it shut now and again."

When we came down to breakfast the next morning, she never mentioned a word about it; it was just like it'd never happened. And we weren't given rabbit's head to eat anymore either; from then on when she cooked rabbit, we got the same as everyone else.

* * * * *

A month or so later, in the early part of 1940, her two sons received their calling up papers, and within a matter of a few short weeks were sent somewhere overseas to fight for their country. Mr. and Mrs. Jones of course knew their call up was inevitable, but when Edwin and Clifford called at the house one day to tell their parents the bad news, the initial shock puts Mrs. Jones in bed for a few days.

As the weeks passed by, Mrs. Jones became more hostile than ever toward Frank and I. Hardly a day went by without her trying to persuade Bryn to contact the billeting officer and get us moved. But Bryn refused to even listen to her. "You don't want to move to another billet do you?" he asked one day when I was on my own. "You do like it here don't you?" I didn't want to upset him so I told him I did. Bryn tried very hard to get his wife to like us, and so did Frank and I, but we never succeeded. In fact, the more we tried, the worse she seemed to get. Her sons liked us though, and we got on very well with them and their wives. Edwin, who watched his father's health very closely, told us one day that it was the best thing that had happened to his father, Frank and I coming to live there.

The moment we'd walk in from school, Bryn's eyes would light up. You could tell he'd been watching the clock all day waiting for us to come in. And once we'd finished our tea, he'd go over to the cupboard where his sons had kept their toys and games. "How about a game of cards after you've finished your tea?" he'd say. Or if we didn't want to play cards, he'd suggest something else, like playing Ludo or Snakes and Ladders. Sometimes we wanted to go out and play in the street with the other kids, but we never said anything, we just stayed in and played with him.

Uncle Clive, Bryn's younger brother, was here the other night. He comes every Tuesday while his wife goes off to some church meeting. We like Uncle Clive, especially when he's telling us some of his Army stories. He forgets and tells us the same stories when he comes the following week, each time more heroic than the last. But I don't care; I still enjoy listening to them.

Whenever I see Uncle Clive he always reminds me of Arthur Askey. He's not only the same height as him, about five foot nothing, but he's got the same shape face, same colour hair, and he wears the same type of horn-rimmed glasses as well. When I first saw Uncle Clive I really thought it was Arthur Askey coming through the door.

But last week when he was here he got so upset with me I thought he was going to get up and leave. He said I was asking him too many personal questions. And I was asking too many questions, but I didn't mean to be nosy or anything. It was just that I was, and still am, interested in other people. Frank nudged me in my side and told me to not be so cheeky and to tell Uncle Clive that I was sorry. I did tell Uncle Clive I was sorry, but I knew when we carried on with the card game that he was still annoyed with me.

After he'd gone, Bryn told me that Uncle Clive always gets very embarrassed when people talk about his height. He said he has done ever since he was a kid. Bryn said I was being far too cheeky by asking Uncle Clive a lot of personal questions. "I only asked him one," I said to Bryn.

"No," he said. "You asked him two. The first one you asked was, did people often get him mixed up with Arthur Askey. That wasn't a very nice thing to say, was it?"

"No it wasn't."

"And then the other question you asked him was why he always has a cigarette in the corner of his mouth and never both- ers to light it. And when he didn't answer you, you kept asking him if you could light it for him. He doesn't smoke Raymond, not any more, hasn't done for years."

"He doesn't smoke?"

"No, he used to. Used to smoke fifty a day, but his

wife made him stop about a year ago. So now he just pretends to smoke; he says it takes the craving away. Personally, if it was me that was married to her, I'd tell her to bugger off and mind her own business."

"Well, why doesn't he tell her to do that?"

"There you go again Raymond, asking too many questions."

"Sorry."

"Because he's terrified of her, that's why, he always has been." "What's she like?"

"Not sure what she looks like now, haven't seen her for years. She doesn't come round anymore."

"Why?"

"Because a long time ago Mrs. Jones and her had a row over something silly, and since then have never spoken to each other."

"Never?"

"No, never. And before you do, don't ask me what the row was over because I'm not going to tell you."

Out of all the games we play, the game that Uncle Clive likes the best is cards. He likes to play with matches and pretend they're real money. He talks a lot as well, and no one gets a word in when he's here. Bryn says as far as talking is concerned, no one can beat his brother. He says talking comes as easy to Uncle Clive as does breathing and farting.

"Why don't you give your mouth a rest?" Bryn says, "At least while you're dealing."

"Don't worry, I won't make a mistake," Uncle Clive says.

"I can deal cards and talk at the same time."

One evening when he was dealing the cards, he lost count and had to start all over again.

"That's because you're talking," Bryn told him. "You're like a bloody old woman."

"It wasn't because I was talking," Uncle Clive says, "I just dropped one that's all." "You can't talk and count at the same time," Bryn tells him, "Not without making a mistake. You're not that bloody clever."

"I used to be able to deal cards and count backwards at one time," Clive says. "When I was in the Army, that is."

"Can you still do it? I ask.

"Yes, of course I can," he says, "but not now, maybe later when we've finished."

When were finished playing and he's standing in the doorway putting his coat on, I ask him again. He pretends he doesn't hear me, and asks Bryn to switch the wireless on so he can listen to the nine o'clock news before he leaves.

"I just want an update on the news to see how our lads are doing before I go," he says.

We all sit around the wireless and listen. The news is not very good, not for the British anyway. That makes Clive mad. He clenches his teeth, "Bloody Germans," he says. "They're just a bunch of bloody sausage stuffers, that's all they are." Bryn asks him to be quiet and not interrupt, but Clive doesn't take any notice.

"And now we've got that Benito bloody Misselloni, or Mussolini, whatever his name is, poking his big bloody nose in, fat, arrogant, little sod. I'd love to give him a kick up his bloody arse as well." Then, when he gets to the scullery door to go out, he comes back into the kitchen, pokes his head around the door and shouts, "Anyway, they've got as much chance of winning this war as I've got of walking on bloody water. I can promise you that."

Viewing The Corpse

It's a Saturday morning and we're getting dressed to go down for our breakfast. Frank has decided to go fishing today. I ask him nicely if he wouldn't mind taking me with him. I have to ask nicely because of what happened last time.

"Yes," he says, to my surprise and amazement. "I'll take you, but there's two conditions."

"I know Frank, no talking and I have to put my own bait on the hook."

"No, you're wrong, these are the conditions. Number one, you have to fish on the opposite bank and not talk. Number two, instead of me emptying the chamber pot today, you have to."

I'm very happy with that arrangement, even though I hate emptying the chamber pot. In fact, I'm so excited to be going fishing, I would have done it all week if he had asked.

So while Frank finishes getting dressed, I grab the chamber pot from under the bed, and carefully make my way very slowly along the landing toward the narrow, creaky stairway. That's the worst part, going down the stairs; you can't see where you're going with a big chamber pot blocking your view. I wait until Frank has gone past me before I start down.

When I get to the fourth or fifth stair, I lose my balance. I have to let go of the chamber pot to grab the banister to prevent myself from falling. I stand frozen as I watch it bounce on every single stair, spraying the contents everywhere. Frank comes rushing into the lobby to see what's happening. Bryn hasn't heard anything because he's got his ear pressed against the wireless trying to tune into the morning news. And Mrs. Jones of course doesn't hear anything, she just carries on doing whatever she's doing in the scullery.

"I tripped Frank" I say, "I couldn't help it."

Frank's eyes are nearly popping out of his head.

"She'll go crazy," he says. "It's all over the carpet and walls." "Will you help me to clean it up before she finds out?"

"How can we?" he says. "She's using the sink in the scullery." "What do you think she'll do to me Frank?"

"I'll take the blame," he says picking up the chamber pot. "It was my job to empty it, not yours."

I sit on the stairs wishing it were all a bad dream.

"Oh no," he says, "its gone all over the clothes on the hall-stand, even on her best hat she wears for church. She'll chuck us out into the street for this lot. "

I rush down to get a closer look.
"She'll kill me for this Frank, what can we do?"

"You better go upstairs out of the way," he says, "and let me do the talking."

She's leaning over the sink in the scullery. Frank taps her on her arm.

"What do you want?" she snarls. "Can't you see I'm busy?" "I want to show you something in the hallway," Frank says. "WHAT? Speak up, can't hear you."

"THE HALLWAY, CAN YOU COME INTO THE HALLWAY?"

She follows him into the hallway shaking her head and mumbling under her breath. I'm at the top of the landing, peeping round the door. She screws her nose up, "Great mother of God, what's the smell?"

"It was an accident," Frank replies meekly. "I'm very sorry about it."

"A what?"

"An accident."

"A WHAT?"

Frank put his mouth to her ear. "AN ACCIDENT, IT WAS AN ACCIDENT."

"Oh, no," she shouts as she realizes what's really happened, "it's gone all over the walls, and all over … Oh Jesus, Mary, and Joseph, it's all over our coats as well."

Bryn comes rushing into the hallway. "What's the matter?"

"I want them both out of this house today," she howls. "Look what he's done; it's everywhere."

Bryn picks up the chamber pot off the floor and examines it. It's not broken, doesn't even have a crack it."

She snatches it from him and says, "You bloody fool, I

don't care about the damn pot; it's what came out of it I'm concerned about."

"Well, it's not going to do any good shouting and bloody screaming at him," Bryn says. "What's done is done, let's get it cleaned up."

"I tripped on the stairs," Frank tells Mrs. Jones, "couldn't see where I was going with the chamber in front of me."

"What?" she says. "What did you say?"

"I COULDN'T SEE THE STAIRS AS I WAS COMING DOWN."

"You stupid boy, you're supposed to empty it into a bucket before you bring it down."

I feel sorry for Frank, just standing there taking all the blame. And even though I don't like my landlady, and I know she hates us, I can't help feeling sorry for her either. I want to go down and tell her how really sorry I am, but I'm too scared. And when I go into the bedroom and look through the window I feel even worse, because down in the middle of the garden Bryn is making a bonfire of all the coats. Well, not all of them, Frank's and mine are still hanging on the back of the kitchen door.

✱ ✱ ✱ ✱ ✱

"For God's sake, will someone open the window, I can't breathe in here." That's what Bryn is shouting as Frank and I walk into the house one day.

It's a Saturday afternoon and we've just come in from the pictures. He's going through one of the worst asthma attacks I've seen him have since we moved here. He's walking around the kitchen with his mouth wide open and his hands around his throat, gasping for air. Frank takes him by the arm and leads him back over to his rocking chair. While he's doing that, I open the scullery door and windows to let some fresh air in. I can hear his laboured breathing, even from the scullery. When I come back into the kitchen, Bryn is slumped in his chair, his head bowed and his arms resting limply over the sides. Frank picks up a newspaper and wafts it in front of his face like Mrs. Jones does sometimes. And when we hear the front door open I run up the lobby to tell her what's happening. She drops her shopping bags and runs into the kitchen.

"In the name of God, what's happened?"

"I think it's one of his attacks," Frank says.

"Yes, I can see that," she says, "but I've never seen him look as bad as this before; we need to get the doctor right away."

Then we see Bryn's eyes open and his lips move. His wife puts her ear to his mouth to listen. "I can't hear what he's saying," she says to Frank. "You try."

Frank puts his ear close to his mouth; he can just about hear him.

"Fetch the doctor quickly." Bryn

says. "What's he saying?"

"He wants the doctor quickly," Frank tells her. "I'll go if you want me to, I know where the surgery is."

"You'll have to run very fast," she says. "It's a long way."

Edwin, Mrs. Jones's son, has applied for a telephone for his mother, at his own expense, but the reason it hasn't come yet is because she's still a long way down on the installation list.

About an hour later the doctor arrives. He examines Bryn and tells him he's very ill and wants him in hospital as soon as possible.

Bryn shakes his head.

"No" he says. "If I'm going to die, doctor, I'll die in my own bed, not in a bloody hospital bed."

"You're not going to die," the doctor says. "I just want you in hospital to check you over."

Bryn keeps shaking his head because he knows the doctor is not being straight with him.

The doctor tries to talk him around. He tells him there's no reason why he shouldn't be out in a few days, But Bryn can see right through the doctor's ploy, and keeps on shaking his head.

"Just get me upstairs to my bed will you, doctor?" Bryn says. "I don't want to go into hospital."

"It's for your own good," Mrs. Jones says. "Do as the doctor tells you."

I can tell by the expression on old Bryn's face that, no matter what anyone says, he isn't about to change his mind. He truly believes that if he does agree to go into hospital, the only way he'll be coming out will be in a wooden box.

The doctor turns to Mrs. Jones shrugs his shoulders and says, "I'm sorry, but there's nothing for it. We'll have to get him upstairs and into bed." Mrs. Jones has tears running down her cheeks as she and the Doctor help him up from his rocking chair and slowly make their way out of the kitchen toward the stairs.

He glances over to where I'm sitting, sees the worried look on my face, gives a weak smile, and says, "I'll be OK; I'll be up in no time."

Later that evening, while Frank is listening to the wireless and Mrs. Jones is busy in the scullery, I sneak out of the kitchen and creep upstairs to Bryn's bedroom. I peep around the door. He's lying on his back looking up at the ceiling. I tap lightly on the door to get his attention. He turns his head, lifts his arm slowly, and waves me over. I pull a chair to the side of his bed and tell him I've just come up to see if he wants anything and to say goodnight. He asks me to stay for a while and talk to him. I want to stay, but I'm scared in case Mrs. Jones comes up and sees me in her bedroom.

"I better go now," I tell him, "so you can get some sleep."

He shakes his head and says don't be frightened, you can stay here, it'll be all right. I sit for a few seconds, wondering what to say, when he turns his eyes from the ceiling to face me.

"What do you want to be when you grow up Raymond?" he asks. "I've never asked you that before."

"I wouldn't mind being a film star," I say. "I've always wanted to be one of those."

"A film star?"

"Yes, a cowboy film star, like Gene Autry."

"And what if you can't get a job as a film star, what then?"

"A cobbler. I'd like to have my own cobbler business like Mr.. Jenkins down the street."

"A cobbler? Why a cobbler?"

"Because I'd like mending shoes."

"Do you think you'd be good at that … good enough to earn a living out of it?"

"Yes, I think so, I've watched him doing it lots of times."

"Well, Raymond, whatever you decide to do, I hope you make the right choice."

"I'm not thinking of going down the mines like you did, not after what you told me."

"Down the mines? No, no, you don't want to go down the mines, otherwise you will finish up like me, and you don't want to do that do you?"

"No, I don't, I'm not going down the mines."

"Do you know what I used to tell my two sons when they were growing up?"

"No."

"Never get a job that will put calluses on your hands and overalls on your back. Do you understand what I'm saying?"

"Yes."

"Good boy. You can go now. I'll see you in the morning."

I have the horrible feeling when I come out of his bedroom that I might never see him alive again. I'm sure he's going to die during the night.

The next morning, before I go downstairs, I peep around his door again. Mrs. Jones has got him propped up to help him breathe easier. He looks even worse than he did last night, pale, drawn and black circles around his eyes. I want to go in and ask him how he's feeling, but I can tell he's asleep by his slower breathing. I try to see him later on in the day, but Mrs. Jones or the doctor is always in there. And it's the same on Sunday as well. I don't even see him then.

The doctor calls again on Monday morning. He's at the house

even before I leave for school today—Bryn must be getting worse.

The moment the four o'clock bell rings, I jump up from my desk and run home as fast as I can. When I walk into the kitchen, Mrs. Jones is sitting at the table holding a hanky to her eyes talking to Frank. She's told him Bryn died peacefully in his sleep just after we left for school this morning. I want to tell her I'm sorry but the lump that comes in my throat makes it difficult for me to speak. "He wanted to die," she tells us. "I know he did. His breathing got so difficult, he couldn't cope with it any longer." Frank says he's sorry and that we'll miss him.

I'm having him laid out in the parlor," she says, "so people can come in and say their last goodbyes. You can both come as well." That frightens me. I loved Bryn like he was my grandfather, but the thought of having to see him lying in a coffin, pale and lifeless, made a shiver go up my spine. I couldn't stop thinking about it all that night and all the next day in school. I told Eddie about it at playtime. I'm sorry I did. "I wouldn't if I was you," he said. "I was made to have one last look at my uncle when he died, and it was terrible. He looked like one of those zombies you see in the pictures."

The following evening after we've finished our tea, Mrs. Jones comes to the kitchen door and tells us to follow her up the hallway. I stay seated and tell Frank I don't want to go. "You have to," he says. "She'll get upset if you don't."

When we get to the parlor, she stands behind me and gently pushes the door open for us to go in. My legs turn to jelly. "Be careful as you go in," Mrs. Jones says. "I don't want anything knocking over."

The candles that have been placed at each end of the coffin are casting eerie shadows across Bryn's face. He lays there all silent with his hands crossed. She's had him dressed in his best pinstripe suit, the one he always wore on their Friday nights out. "He looks peaceful doesn't he?" she says, brushing his hair from his forehead. "That's because he's not suffering any more, you see."

The next day we walk to the graveyard behind a horse-drawn hearse, and as we pass the houses, people stand, heads bowed and motionless. All you can hear is the clip-clop of the horse's hooves. When we get to the graveyard, I watch them lower Bryn's coffin into his grave. The vicar says that Bryn will be enjoying life in heaven now, so don't worry about him. He says we'll all see him again because when we die we'll all meet up again in heaven. He says people live forever in heaven. I'd like to live forever down here, I say to myself. I don't want to die and get buried in a hole. In fact, I don't ever want to go to another funeral as long as I live.

"Stealing" Candy From The Pantry

A few weeks later Frank went to see Mrs. Davis, our billeting officer, to ask if she can find us a new billet. When she asks him why, Frank tells her it's because he broke into the pantry. He tells her Mrs. Jones wants him out as quick as possible. Mrs. Davis is confused and asks him what he's talking about. "I broke in to the pantry to get our candies back," he says. "She took them from us and locked them in there."

"Candies?" Mrs. Davis asks. "What do you mean, candies? What are they?"

"They are sweets," Frank tells her. "American sweets from the American Red Cross, that's what they call them over there."

"Why did she confiscate them?" Mrs. Davis asks. "What had you been doing for her to take them from you?"

"Nothing, we've done nothing wrong," Frank says. "We only had one sweet each when she took them from us."

Mrs. Davis isn't sure whether Frank is telling the truth.

"I don't know what to believe," she says. "It seems very strange to me why she would she want to take your sweets away from you."

Frank shrugs his shoulders and tells her he doesn't know either.

* * * * *

Although Frank tried every way possible that day to persuade me to climb into the pantry, I'd already made up my mind that it wasn't going to be me. I'd decided that this time, no matter what he says, I'm going to stick to my guns and not give in. Mrs. Jones didn't even allow her husband in there, never mind anyone else. But rather than refuse Frank (which I knew would be pointless anyway), I thought it would be a better idea to convince him I was too small to reach the opening above the door.

"I can't reach that high, Frank; I'm too small."

"You can," he says, sliding a chair against the door and pulling me toward it. "It's easy, just stand on the chair, grab the windowsill, and pull yourself up."

"No, you do it Frank, you're much taller than me."

Frank gets agitated and annoyed with me. "I won't fit through that small space stupid, do as you're told and get up on the chair and climb in. She'll be back soon."

Frank knows that he can fit through the window just as well as I can, but like me, he doesn't want to get caught in there either. "It's no good Frank," I say, pretending I can't reach. "You'll have to do it, I can't reach."

He grabs hold of my arm and pulls me back onto the chair again. "I've told you," he says, "the window's much too small for me to fit through."

I get back on the chair again, stand on tiptoe and stretch my arm a little higher this time, not as high as I'm able to, just a little higher. "No, Frank," I say, "I can't reach it."

"Get out of the way," he says, dragging me off the chair, "and keep a look out for her. I'll do it myself."

He's up on the chair and through the window in a few seconds, and it's not until he drops to the floor on the other side that he suddenly realizes he can't get out as easy as he got in. "OH NO," he shouts. "How am I going to get out? I can't reach the window from in here."

I don't say anything. I'm just glad it's him that's locked in there and not me. He shouts for me to look for something for him to stand on. I say OK, and pretend I'm looking around.

"There might be something in the shed," he says. "Try in there ... and hurry up."

I open and close the scullery door and pretend I've gone to the shed. "I can't find anything in the shed either Frank. Have you found the sweets yet?"

"SWEETS? I don't care about the sweets; I want to get out of here before she gets back. You and your bloody sweets, you greedy little thing, that's all you're worried about."

I'm shocked to hear Frank swearing again.

"That's a bad word," I say. "Mam will go mad if she finds out you're using swear words."

Suddenly the box of sweets comes flying out of the pantry window and lands on the floor in front of me. "SHURRUP!" he shouts. "I can swear if I want to. Take them upstairs before she gets back."

"Where shall I put them?"

"Hide them on top of the wardrobe, she can't see up there."

"OK, Frank."

"And you better not eat any while you're up there, otherwise you know what will happen."

I already have one tucked in my cheek. "No, Frank," I shout. "I won't."

When I come down he tells me to stay in the hallway so I can keep an eye on the front door; that way I can let him know when Mrs. Jones arrives. The door into the pantry is on the left wall at the end of the lobby, just before you enter the kitchen. I lean my back on the wall opposite the pantry door, slide down to the floor and draw my knees up to my chin and wait. After a few more attempts of trying to jump up to the window, he somehow manages to get one foot on the door latch on the inside and one hand on the window ledge. He puffs and pants trying to pull himself up. The door latch breaks off and brings him crashing back to the floor again. "Oh Jesus," he shouts. "I've broken the door latch, now I'll never get out of here."

I ask him if he's hurt himself. "Never mind that," he says. "What are you eating? I can hear you chewing something."

"I'm not Frank, not chewing anything."

"You are, you bloody liar! You're eating one of those candies."

With one in my hand and another in my mouth, "No, Frank," I say. "Honest, I'm not."

A few minutes later I hear the key turn in the front door, so I make a dash for the bedroom. "She's here Frank," I shout as I head for the stairs. "She's coming in now."

Mrs. Jones nearly had a heart attack when she opened the

pantry door that day and saw Frank inside. She got such a shock that she dropped the bag of groceries all over the floor and screamed so loud you could have heard her in the next street. She flopped into one of the chairs in the kitchen saying, "Oh God! Oh God! I thought it was a burglar." Then, when she got her breath back, she told Frank he had three days to find a new billet or he'd be out on his backside in the street.

* * * * *

Later that week Mrs. Davis calls at Frank's school to tell him she's found him a new billet, and that his new landlady says he can move in whenever he likes. Frank asks if he can move in that evening. "You can," she says, "as long as you're ready when I come to pick you up at the house." Frank's new billet is close to where Mam lives, which means he can see her whenever he wants to now, every day if he prefers.

When I arrive home from school at 4:30, Frank is already sat at the kitchen table with his haversack and gas mask over his shoulder. I get excited and ask him where our new billet is.

"They only have enough room for one," he says. "I'm sorry, but you have to stay here."

"Don't leave me here with her Frank," I say. "Ask Mrs. Davis to take me as well, please, Frank, please."

He puts his arm around my shoulder. "Don't worry," he says, "she's promised to find you a place as soon as possible. You'll be out of here in a few days."

It's around 6 p.m. when Mrs. Davis finally arrives. Frank has been in a panic thinking she wasn't coming. He jumps up when he hears the knock on the front door, and goes in the hallway to check if it's her. Mrs. Jones comes out of the parlor to let her in.

When the billeting officer steps inside, she apologizes to Mrs. Jones for forgetting to go round the back. She's told it doesn't matter and is lead through to the kitchen.

Mrs. Jones doesn't say goodbye to Frank, doesn't even look at him, just turns away and disappears back into the parlor. He comes over to the table where I'm sitting to say goodbye.

"Mrs. Davis has told me she'll get you out of here as soon as possible," he says, "and when she does, she's promised she'll try and get you near to where I live."

I nod my head and say OK. Then just as he's about to close the door, he comes back.

"I've moved the box of sweets from the top of my wardrobe to yours," he says. "I've just taken a couple for myself, so you can have the rest."

I nod again.

"I'll come back and see you at the weekend. Maybe we'll go fishing."

Sometime later Mrs. Jones emerges from the parlor to get my dinner from the oven. She doesn't say anything, just plonks it down on the table and disappears again. For a while, I sit picking at it until I eventually push the plate away and go upstairs to my bedroom. I climb on a chair and get the candies from the top of the wardrobe and lay on the bed, crying and munching. After a while I begin to feel sick, so I get up and go back downstairs. I sit in Bryn's rickety rocking chair in front of the fire and switch the wireless on. I twiddle the dial to find something interesting to listen to, but there are just a lot of whistling and whining sounds coming from it. Then when I do get a station through, all they're talking about is the war. I give the dial one last turn before I switch it off and hear the faint sound of Vera Lynn singing one of my favourite songs, "The White Cliffs of Dover." I can hardly hear her, so I twiddle the dial a bit more and manage to get it a little louder and clearer, and although there's still a lot of interference, I am able to hear the rest of the song before I finally lose the station altogether.

> There'll be blue birds over
>
> The white cliffs of Dover
>
> Tomorrow just you wait and see.
>
> There'll be love and laughter
>
> And peace ever after
>
> Tomorrow when the world is free.

I switch the wireless off and think how great it would be if the war would finish tomorrow just like the song says. I'd be able to go home and live with Mam and Dad and my sisters and brothers again. I wouldn't be an evacuee anymore. There would be plenty of food to eat and we would be back in our nice house on Brookbridge Road again.

I rock backward and forward wondering what to do with myself. I keep wishing Bryn and Frank were here. I glance over at the empty table and visualize the three of us sitting round, laughing and joking, playing one of the games we used to play. Then the laughing and joking stops, and Bryn and Frank disappear. It's all silent again. Except for the incessant ticking of the pendulum clock on the wall that is, ticking the meaningless hours away.

As usual, on the stroke of eight Mrs. Jones comes into the kitchen to tell me to go to bed. I don't want her to see I've been crying, so I cover my face with my comic. She picks my plate up off the table to take it into the scullery.

"What's the matter with your dinner?" she asks. "I don't feel hungry," I reply.

"You'll not get anything else until tomorrow" she says, as she takes my plate into the scullery. "So you better make up your mind if you're going to eat it or not, otherwise it goes in the bin."

"No, thank you," I say. "I'm not hungry."

I lay in bed feeling very sorry for myself. I keep thinking how lucky Frank is, now that he doesn't have to live with Mrs. Jones anymore.

And as the days and weeks slowly creep by, and he doesn't come to see me like he promised he would, the self-pity begins to change into bitterness, bitterness toward my mother for sending me away in the first place. Sending me away to live with strangers, strangers that don't want me in their homes. What are we all doing here, I keep asking myself, why didn't we just stay in Liverpool in our nice new house.

It was just as well I wasn't able to see into the future that night, because when I did eventually move into a new billet, things were to become far worse than anything I could imagine.

Grenade Games Turn To Grief

Frank did eventually come round to see me. It was on a Saturday afternoon when Mrs. Jones was out shopping. He came to tell me all about his new billet, and take me to the pictures. It made me feel guilty about being bitter toward him. After all, I thought, who could blame him for wanting to get out of that house. He said that being an evacuee, the local kids had given him a bad time when he first moved in. But once he'd beaten the gang leader in a pre-arranged fist fight, they all became good friends.

He was living in a billet on the other side of town, close to my mother's billet. He liked it there now that he could visit Mam every day. And not only that, the people he lived with were really nice people, the kind that went out of their way to make him feel at home. In later years, when the conversation came up about the evacuation, he told me how very lucky he thought he was to get to live in such a nice place. The boy that was supposed to go there instead of him got scabies and was suddenly sent into hospital. It was so nice, he said, it was nothing less than a child's paradise.

He lived not far from the coast, in a place where all the kids would go down to do some fishing in the tin canoes they'd expertly made from the spare metal sheets that were lying about from the tin works. His new friends also taught him how to trap fish under his feet, and how to spear them with metal spears they made. His constant companion, he said, was a small, stray, mongrel dog he befriended when he was walking along the beach one day. He called her Peggy-peg-leg because she limped when she walked. She followed him everywhere, even in the water. When Frank asked his landlady if he could keep the dog, she said she didn't mind as long as he made a kennel for her. She didn't want Peggy fighting with her cat. So Peggy had to sleep in the coal shed for the first few nights until Frank's landlady's son made the dog a kennel.

But Peggy was already an old dog when her and Frank first met up. And as time went on, Frank noticed her getting weaker and weaker. She couldn't keep up with him like she used to. He'd have to wait every few yards for her to catch up. One afternoon when he came home from school, he saw her lying in the middle of the garden. As he got closer, he knew there was something wrong because she didn't even lift her head up to look at him. He picked her up and laid her down in her kennel. She died the next day. It took Frank a long time to get over Peggy's death.

★ ★ ★ ★ ★

Frank liked it so much where he was living that he stayed there until we left to go home at the end of the war. Besides Peggy dying, the only other bad memory he has of those days was when he and his friends came across a hand grenade lying in the field one day.

It was a highly fenced field where the Home Guard did their training. Frank knew that he and his friends shouldn't have been anywhere near there. There were notices all along the fence saying it was strictly out of bounds to the public. But Trevor, one of his friends, said he always played there, and no one ever bothered him. He thought it was the ideal place for playing war games. Trevor showed them a secret hole in the fence that only he knew about. When they climbed through, he suggested they look in the grass and collect the spent shells. There were so many lying about, their pockets were bulging with them in no time. Then suddenly, one of the boys shouted for everyone to come and see what he had found. They all gathered in a circle and looked down.

"Do you think it's a real one?" Trevor asked as he kneeled down to pick it up. They all shook their heads in silence. They'd never seen a hand grenade before, especially that close up. The others told Trevor to put it down in case it was real. "What are you scared of," Trevor said. "It's probably only a dummy; they don't use real ones." The others disagreed and told him that it might not be a dummy, and to put it back on the ground, but unfortunately he didn't take their advice. He started throwing it up like a ball and catching it. The others got frightened, backed away, and headed for the hole in the fence. When they were on the other side of the fence, they shouted and told him to put it down and come out. But he wouldn't. He just ignored their warnings and carried on playing with it. So they decided to walk away in the hope he would put it down and follow them. They were only a short distance from the field when they heard a mighty explosion. By the time they got back, there were Army personnel running onto the field, and people running up to the fence to see what had happened. A few minutes later an ambulance arrived. When they were carrying the stretcher out of the field, Frank squeezed into the crowd and up to one of the ambulance men to ask if Trevor was all right. But he didn't bother asking, he knew that when they covered your head with a blanket, you were dead.

* * * * *

It's a Saturday morning. I'm sitting by the fire reading a comic when Mrs. Jones calls me. I walk up the hallway and see her in the dining room, sitting by the fire, resting her foot on a chair. I knock.

"You can come in," she says. "Don't just stand there." When I go in she hands a shopping basket to me.

"I've done something to my ankle," she says, "so you'll have to do the shopping today. Do you think you can do that?"

"Don't know. I've never done shopping before."

"Well, I'm getting too old to be standing in queues all day anyway, so you'll just have to learn. Your legs are much younger than mine."

"How will I know what to ask for?"

"Don't worry about that," she says. "I'll give you a note which will have a list of all the things I need. Just go into the kitchen and get your cap and coat while I get everything ready."

When I go back into the dining room she tells me to pick up the bag and look inside.

"There's a ration book in there," she says. "Do you see it?" "Yes."

"Good—don't lose it whatever you do." "What do I do with it?"

"I'm going to tell you now, just listen carefully. All you have to do when you get to the baker's and the butcher's is give them the note that's in the purse with the money and the ration book. They'll know what to do then."

"A purse? I have to carry a purse with me? Can't I put the money and the note in my pocket instead?"

"You'll do as you're told," she snaps back. "And don't be cheeky. You'll carry the money in the purse, not in your pocket."

"Why?"

"Because otherwise you'll lose the money, that's

why." "But only girls have purses, someone might see

me." "Do as you're told, keep the money in the

PURSE." "Yes, Mrs. Jones."

"If I find you've taken the money out of the purse and put it in your pocket, you'll be in very serious trouble. Do you understand?"

"Yes, Mrs. Jones."

I'm about to close the dining room door ... "And don't forget what I told you about the bread, make sure it's fresh. Because if you don't, you know what will happen, you'll go all the way back with it, do you hear me?"

"Yes, Mrs. Jones, I hear you."

As soon as I'm round the corner, I take the money and notes out of the purse and put them in my pocket. *Nobody's going to see me carrying a purse, especially one of the girls from our school.*

The queue is long but moving quite steadily. When I finally get to the counter, I hand the note to one of the assistants. She shakes her head when she reads it, and then hands it to her boss, the baker.

When the baker reads it and sees that Mrs. Jones has under-
lined and capitalized the word <u>FRESH</u> on the note, he gets
extremely angry. He glares at me with clenched teeth and begins
to rip the note up into tiny pieces. And when he's satisfied he
can't get the pieces any smaller, and he's put them in a small
paper bag and stuffed the bag in my jacket pocket, he bends down
and shouts in my face,. "Doesn't that lady ever stop complaining?
You give that note back to her sonny and tell her that the bread is
always fresh from here. She gets it straight out of the oven just
like everyone else does."

I'm so embarrassed with him shouting at me, and all the
customers staring at me, I decide to turn tail and run out the shop
as fast as I can. But I only get halfway up the street when I realize I've left the shopping bag behind. *It's got the ration books in
it. If I go home without them, I'll have to go back.*

When I get back to the shop, the baker is standing in the doorway looking up and down the street.

"I've left the bag in the shop," I tell him. "Please can I have it
back? The ration books are in it."

"Come in," he says. "I'm sorry if I frightened you. I didn't
mean to; she gets me so annoyed, that woman."

He's a very tall, stick-thin man with a bald head and big, black,
bushy eyebrows. He lifts me up and sits me on the counter next
to the glass cake cabinet. Then, with both hands on his knees, he
bends forward and asks me my name.

"Raymond Evans." I tell him, my eyes fixed firmly on the
cakes inside the cabinet. "And where do you live Raymond?"

"I live with Mrs. Jones by the cobbler's shop on Black-
stock Street."

"Oh," he says, with a surprised look on his face. "So you live
with Mrs. Jones, do you?"

"Yes, but only because of the war. She's not my real mother, I'm an evacuee from Liverpool, you see."

"Oh, now I understand," he says. "That's why I've never seen you in here before. How long have you lived with Mrs. Jones then?"

"Since last year September, about ten months."

"I see, and how do you like living in Llanelli then Raymond?" "It's alright, but I'd rather be back in Liverpool with my Mam
and Dad and my sisters and brothers."

He opens the glass door on the cake stand. "Would you like one of those Raymond? Those cakes inside there?"

"Yes, please."

"Help yourself then," he says. "Take anyone you like."

After I've picked the biggest cream bun in the cabinet, he lifts me down and hands me the shopping bag.

"The loaf's inside with your ration books," he says. "I'm sorry I shouted at you, it's not your fault."

I look inside to double check the ration books are there.

"Will we see you again Raymond," he asks as I make my way to the door.

"Yes," I tell him. "You will see me again, because from now on I'll be doing all the messages."

* * * * *

Arriving home from my usual messages a few Saturdays later, Mrs. Jones comes into the kitchen carrying a loaf in her hand. The same loaf that I've just brought in from the baker's a few minutes ago. "That's not today's," she says, plonking it on my lap. "It's yesterday's, I can tell by the feel of it. So get your skates and take it back to him right now and get a fresh one. And when you see him, you can tell from me that if I don't get a fresh one, it's the last time I'll be buying anything in his shop again."

"But it is fresh Mrs. Jones, it was still warm when he gave it me. It's just that it's gone cold that's all."

"No, it's not," she says. "You're just saying that so you won't have to go back with it."

"I'm not, Mrs. Jones, honest. It is today's."

"No, it's not," she says, "and don't argue with me. I know a fresh loaf when I see it. Take it back right now."

"I don't know what to say to him, Mrs. Jones, will you give me a note?"

"No, you don't need a note, just tell him I said it's not fresh, that's all."

What am I going to say to him, I keep asking myself as I make my way back to the baker's. I know it was fresh when he gave it to me; he'll go mad. I wished she'd given me a note.

When I get to the shop I peer through the window to see if he's in the bakery at the back or serving behind the counter. When I see he's not behind the counter, I dash inside and join the queue, keeping my eyes peeled on the door that leads into the bakery, in case he suddenly appears. When it finally comes to my turn to be served, the bakery door opens and in he walks.

"Hello Raymond, back again I see, what is it this time?"

I'm so shocked at seeing him that I'm completely lost for words. "Err, I can't remember," I tell him, making a hasty retreat to the door. "I must have left the note behind. I'll be back later." I pull the door behind me and hotfoot it up the street.

Now I'm in a Catch-22 situation—I'm on my way home with the same loaf in my bag. *I'll just have to make her believe he did change the loaf.*

She takes it out of the bag and gives it a squeeze. "Is this a fresh one? Doesn't feel like it."

"Oh, yes, Mrs. Jones, this is definitely a fresh one, it came out of the oven this morning; he told me it did."

"Ah," she says, "so I was right, the other one was a yesterday's loaf."

"Yes, it was, but he did tell me to tell you he's very, very sorry about it, about getting it mixed up with the other stale loaves, that is. He told me to tell you he'll make sure it doesn't ever happen again. "

"I should think so, too," she says. "He must think I've just come over on a banana boat."

* * * * *

It was no wonder the old lady was always complaining about queuing; in those days there were always long queues in all the shops, no matter what time of the day you happened to go. This was especially true in the food shops. Some of the queues were so long, that it was difficult to know which shop the queue was for.

I didn't mind doing the shopping, I quite enjoyed it really; it was just the time I spent in the queues. And the shops that always had the longest queues, especially on Saturdays, were the fish and chip shops. I'm sure the entire population of Llanelli ate fish and chips for their dinners on Saturdays. It didn't matter what the weather was like, it could be pouring down with rain, or blowing a blizzard, they had to have their fish and chips.

I've just joined the chip shop queue on a Saturday, dinner time after a busy morning doing the shopping. It's just beginning to rain. The queue, as usual, stretches out of the shop and along the pavement. I do think of running back for my cap and raincoat, but that would mean I'll lose my place in the queue, and I don't want to do that. I keep wishing the man next to me would open up his umbrella so I could share it with him. (I often squeeze under someone's umbrella when it is raining.) But because he's wearing a raincoat and trilby, and the rain at this point isn't heavy enough to warrant using his umbrella, he just stands with it hooked over his arm whistling lowly to himself.

I keep staring up at him, hoping he might feel sorry for me and offer to lend it me. Unfortunately, it doesn't work. He just keeps looking straight ahead pretending I'm not there.

When the rain starts to get heavier, I'm tempted to give up and go home, but I know by doing that I won't get anything to eat until teatime. To make matters worse, one of the fryers is not working today, so they are much slower serving than normal, consequently making the queue move at a snail's pace.

I envy the people in the front of the queue who are out of the rain and in the warmth of the shop. Why won't he lend me his umbrella, he's not using it. Maybe if I ask him nice he'll lend me it. I tug his sleeve.

"Excuse me, sir, could I borrow your umbrella, please?"

He doesn't even look at me, just keeps looking straight ahead without saying a word.

"Excuse me, sir, but ... "

"We'll be out of the rain shortly," he snaps back. "You don't need the umbrella, we're nearly inside now."

The man who's standing in front turns around. "Lend him it

for God's sake," he says. "He's getting drenched."

This gets the man with the umbrella very annoyed. He tells the man in front to mind his own business, and that it has nothing to do with him. An argument breaks out until eventually the umbrella man gives in and very reluctantly shoves the umbrella into my hand. But he does it with a very stern warning that if I break it, I'll have to pay for it.

I'd never used an umbrella before, so I have no idea how to open it. After struggling for a while, I ask him if he wouldn't mind opening it for me. With a foul look on his face, and muttering under his breath, he snatches the umbrella out of my hand and pushes it open in such a flurry, that if I hadn't ducked out of the way, it would have certainly given me a fair clout on the back of my head. This starts another argument between him and the man in front again, and very quickly develops into a pushing and shoving match.

I pick the umbrella up off the ground, and back away from the scuffle. By this time, the rain is so heavy it's literally bouncing off the umbrella. I stand under it watching the two men still shoving and pushing each other. I notice that the proprietor of the fish and chip shop and some of his customers have now come out of the shop to see what all the commotion is about.

I then do something that's against all the laws of queuing. While everyone's attention is taken up by what's going on outside the chip shop, I sneak inside and get served by one of the proprietor's young assistants. When I come out, the proprietor is sandwiched between the two men, having a very hard time trying keeping them apart.

I can't help feeling sorry for the umbrella man at this point. In fact, I begin to feel quite guilty about the whole thing. After all, if I'd gone home in the first place and got my cap and raincoat, all of this wouldn't have happened. Anyway, there's nothing I can do about it now, and because the rain is coming down sideways, and my fish and chips are getting cold, I ask a lady in the queue if she would hand the umbrella back to the owner when they finished fighting.

"It's that man's there," I tell her. "The one that's wearing the raincoat and trilby."

It was not unusual to find ordinance littering the countryside after an enemy plane had been shot down on its way to or from a bombing mission.

Hero To Scoundrel

In Sixty Seconds

As you may have gathered by now, Mrs. Jones was a notoriously fussy housekeeper. Without exaggerating, one could guarantee on any given day that not one tiny speck of dust could be found in this lady's house. She was so incredibly fussy that she had a strict time schedule for every single chore, no matter how tiny it was. Hail, rain, or snow, her first job (not once a week, like everyone else, but every single morning) was to polish the outside brass. First the doorknocker, then the brass number on the top of door, and finally the tiny brass ring around the bell push. When she'd finished those three things, she'd go down on her knees and scrub the daylights out of her three red-tiled steps. And because of her tight schedule she'd get extremely annoyed with herself if she hadn't completed those jobs by the time the nine o'clock morning news came on the wireless. It wasn't because she was interested in listening to the news, far from it; it was her schedule she was worried about—nothing was allowed to alter that.

When she'd finished outside, and because she didn't want to stand on her clean steps, she'd pull the front door closed, empty the bucket of water in the gutter, and walk all the way round to the back and come in the house via the scullery door.

"You're bloody crazy, woman," Bryn had shouted to her one day as she passed him in the kitchen. "Polishing brass and washing bloody steps every single day; everybody else on the street only does theirs once a week."

"What I do in this house," she said, "has nothing to do with neighbors or anyone else in this street. I like to keep my house clean."

Her next job was to take all the coats off the hallstand so she could give the mirror and woodwork a good polishing. Then, at 9:45, she'd begin to polish all the brass ornaments around the kitchen fireplace. And so it went on, every morning, day after day. She'd throw a fit if something upset her schedule. The world was at war, Britain was being flattened every night by German bombs, and yet all you could get out of my landlady was, "Good gracious, look at the time. Five past nine already and I haven't finished the outside brass yet."

* * * * *

To allow the local council enough time to find places in the surrounding schools, a couple of temporary classrooms were set up in the vestry of St. Peter's Church.

I never made it to the top of the class in school. The reason being that if I didn't like the lesson, I'd simply switch off and let my imagination take me to far more interesting places. Having said that, I did excel in a couple of things, arithmetic being one of them, and composition another. In fact, it was only arithmetic and composition I was ever given three stars for. Miss Albright took us in those lessons; she was my favourite teacher.

Now Miss Grainger, on the other hand, that's a different story. She doesn't like me at all. She says all I ever do is talk in class and moan about my billet. She says that she's fed up with me complaining about my billet all the time and wishes she could have me sent back to Liverpool, out of her sight.

Miss Grainger is very tall for a lady, at least six foot, if not more. Eddie Rathbone, he's my best mate, says he's never seen a lady so tall. He says it's probably the reason why she's never been married. He says men don't marry women taller than themselves because they get bossed about. I tell him I wouldn't marry her anyway, even if she were only four foot tall.

My first major encounter with Miss Grainger was a result of my refusal to join in with the rest of the class in learning how to knit. It was on a Friday afternoon, normally the part of the week when we were allowed to choose what we wanted to do, such as playing with Plasticine, or painting and drawing. But this Friday afternoon was to be different, same as the following Friday afternoon would be, and the one after that, and the one after that as well. It was one of those Friday afternoons that I was to be judged as an academic failure just because I refused to knit.

As soon as we'd all settled down behind our desks after playtime, Miss Grainger and one of the prefects comes around giving out balls of knitting wool and knitting needles. They start at the front of the class; Eddie and I are sat at the back.

Eddie taps me on the shoulder. "We're all getting knitting needles and wool," he says. "Not just the girls, but the boys as well."

I don't believe him. I think he's kidding me. "Knitting? The boys? I don't believe you."

"It's true," he says. "She wants everyone to learn how to knit."

"Everyone? The boys as well?"

"Everyone, honest."

I still don't believe him, so I stand up to get a better look. That's when I see the prefect plonk a big ball of navy wool and a pair of knitting needles on Georgie Mathews' desk. I stand for a few seconds longer hoping the prefect will go back to his desk and tell him she'd made a mistake and that she should have given it to the girl behind him. But she doesn't, she just carries on, making her way up toward Eddie and me. Then Miss Grainger turns around and sees me standing.

"Sit down, Raymond Evans," she shouts. "Don't worry, there's enough for everyone."

Enough for everyone. I don't care if you've got enough for the whole school, I don't want any." I think to myself.

When they finish giving the wool out, Miss Grainger stands in front of the class with a pair of knitting needles in her hand and gives a short demonstration on how to "knit one and pearl one."

"It's quite simple," she says. "You'll soon get the hang of it." Eddie puts his hand up. "What are we going to knit, miss?"

I turn around to look at him. I can't believe he's asking such a question.

"A scarf," she says. "Navy ones for the boys and white ones for the girls. You've got plenty of time to have them finished before we break up for the holiday in a few weeks."

What really shocks me is to see the delight on Eddie's face when he manages to get his first row of stitches on his needle. My best friend Eddie, sitting there behind his desk like some old Granny knitting, and in front of all the girls as well.

"It's easy," he keeps telling me. "I'll show you if you want."

"Show me? No thanks," I tell him. "I'm not learning how to knit for her or anyone else."

"You'll get yourself into trouble if you don't try."

"I don't care," I say. "I'll just tell her I don't want to do it. And anyway if my Dad finds out I'm knitting in school, what's he going to think about it? His son learning to knit."

A few weeks later when everyone has nearly finished their scarves, Miss Grainger comes over to where I am sitting, snatches the needles from my hand, opens my desk, and throws them inside.

"Except for you, Raymond Evans," she says, "everyone in the class will have finished their scarves by next week, and yet here's you with only half a row of stitches on your needles."

I don't say anything, just nod and say, "Yes, miss."

"So today, in order for you to try and catch up, you'll stay back after school and do some knitting."

Everyone in the class, including Billy Johnson who sits next to me, starts sniggering.

When everyone has gone home, Miss Grainger sits at her desk marking books while I struggle with my knitting. I'm all fingers and thumbs trying to knit as fast as I can. Every time I manage to get a few stitches on the needle, they somehow fall off again. An hour later when she's finished marking the books, she comes over. I can't remember exactly how many, but I've somehow managed to get five or six full rows completed. I'm amazed at what I've accomplished in such a short time. But it doesn't make any difference to Miss Grainger, I can tell by the look on her face when she picks it up.

"You're hopeless," she says, as she drags it all apart. "You're not even trying."

I stare in disbelief at the empty needles lying on my desk. An hour's work gone in a flash. I politely ask what could be possibly wrong with it; after all, it looks perfectly all right to me.

"Holes" she says. "It's full of holes."

"Holes? I don't know what you mean, miss."

She bends down with her face nearly touching mine and narrows her eyes. "HOLES," she repeats. "You're dropping stitches all the time making HOLES."

I'm told to put my coat on and go home. That's good, I think to myself, that's the end of my knitting lessons; she's finally given it up as a bad job. When I get to the door she tells me to go back to my desk and pick up my knitting needles and wool I take them home with me. She tells me that instead of playing out in the street each evening, I can spend the time working on my scarf. She says it will give me plenty of time to have at least half the scarf done before next week's knitting lesson.

"Mark my words, Raymond Evans," she says, as I walk out of the classroom. "I'm going to have you knit that scarf if it's the last thing you ever do."

That evening after my tea, I take the knitting needles and wool out of the paper bag, walk up the lobby, and knock on the parlor door.

"I've got to knit a scarf," I tell my landlady, "but I don't know how to do it. Can you show me?"

She picks the wool up and examines it. For a brief moment I think she's actually going to offer to do it for me. "If you can't do it yourself," she says, "why don't you ask your sister to knit it for you?"

"Elsie, of course, why didn't I think of that?

I strutted into the classroom the following Friday not with half a scarf around my neck, but with a completed scarf around my neck.

Miss Grainger comes over before I have time to sit down.

"You didn't knit this Raymond Evans."

"I did, miss, no one helped me. I did it all on my own, honest, miss."

Just then one of the girls puts her hand up. "He didn't, miss," she shouts. "He's telling fibs. His sister Elsie knitted it for him. I saw him go round to her house with it."

"She's lying, miss. I did do it all on my own."

"All right then," the teacher says. "We'll get you some needles and you can show everyone how good you've become with your knitting."

Of course, I have no alternative but to own up, which results in me becoming the laughing stock of the classroom. I was given some new wool and told to start knitting.

* * * * *

As an evacuee, escape for me was never a real possibility. The only possible way I thought I could get back to Liverpool was by walking along the railway tracks. I often used those tracks for a shortcut from school, especially when it was raining; it cut the journey practically in half. Sometimes I used to stand in the middle of the tracks and gaze into the distance wondering how far Liverpool really was. I'd pretend I was looking through a pair of binoculars and that I could see our house on Brookbridge Road.

There were warning signs everywhere about going on the railway tracks. There was even a big one on the wall in our classroom. But they didn't deter me; even though the Home Guard and the police kept a close eye on the area, I just hated that long walk home. But I was very careful about it. Before I attempted to go anywhere near the embankment, I always had a good look up and down the street to make sure there was no one around.

There were only two other people that knew I went on the railway tracks. Eddie was one and Georgie Mathews was the other. The problem was, besides being the teacher's pet, Georgie Mathews loved snitching on people. But luckily I caught him before he had a chance to tell Miss Grainger about it. I didn't hit him, I just warned him that he'd be thrown over the church wall into the prickly bushes if he did decide to snitch on me.

Just a few, short weeks later, the German air force began a series of bombing attacks over Britain, later known as the Battle of Britain. But the Germans, as much as they tried, never did achieve complete control of the air. And that was, of course, because of the Royal Air Force.

Swansea, which was about twelve miles from Llanelli, was one of the many major cities that suffered extensive bombing by the Germans. After each air raid, before returning to Germany, the German pilots would indiscriminately jettison any bombs they had left. It didn't matter to them where they landed, just as long as they got rid of them. Some of those bombs landed on Llanelli, and one of them, which happened to be an unexploded bomb, landed me in a lot of trouble.

I was on my way home from school taking the usual short-cut, when I saw it lying on the ground between the railway lines. Keeping a safe distance, I stood transfixed for a while just staring at it. I couldn't understand how a bomb could drop all the way from the sky, and yet not explode. Although it wasn't uncommon to find unexploded bombs after an air raid, I'd never come across one before.

After a few minutes I plucked up enough courage to bend down and take a closer look. I was very careful not to get too close, there were signs everywhere warning you not to go near unexploded bombs. Once I'd had a good look at it, I turned round and ran down the embankment as fast as I could to report it to an ARP warden or a policeman. Luckily I was only a short distance from the police station, so I headed straight there.

On the way, it suddenly occurred to me that if a train came before the police had time to get back and remove the bomb, the train could be blown up. Whether this particular bomb was a real danger to the train, I've no idea, but at the time, after seeing soldiers in the cinema laying dynamite on railway lines and blowing trains up every day, I thought it was. Anyway, the more I thought about it, the more I was convinced I should go back, pick it up, and save the next train from being blown up. But although the blowing up of the train was the major reason why I went back, I had another reason. I was sure an act as brave as that would probably get my name in the local newspapers. Albert had told me once that a kid in his class got his name in the papers, and that was just for reporting he'd found a bomb, not for actually taking it to the police station himself.

I began to visualize the morning's headline:

RAYMOND EVANS, A VERY BRAVE EVACUEE FROM LIVERPOOL,
PREVENTS TRAIN FROM BEING BLOWN UP;
THOUSANDS AND THOUSANDS OF LIVES SAVED.

I look around to make sure there's no one about, then very gently slide my hands underneath, lift it up, hold it against my chest, and head for the police station. I've only walked a few yards when my arms feel like they are being torn from my shoulders. I have to stop outside of a house even after only a short distance and sit down on their garden wall for a rest. And as I sit there a boy comes out of the house opposite and looks over and sees the bomb resting across my knees. For a few seconds he stands frozen to the doorstep with his mouth wide open, then he steps back in, and quickly closes the door just enough to show his face and shouts, "Hey! Is that a real bomb you've got there?"

"Yes."

"Where are you going with it?"

"To the police station. It's a German one. I found it on the railway track."

He slams the door shut and goes into the parlor and peers at me through the window. I get up and walk a bit further until I have to stop for another rest. And that's what I have to keep doing until I get to the police station.

It's one of those little country police stations that is run by a senior officer, a couple of sergeants, and half a dozen or more constables. When I get inside I walk up to a desk where a sergeant is busy writing. "Excuse me, sir," I say. "Where do you want me to put this?"

"Put what?" he asks, not lifting his head up to look at me. "What have you got there, sonny?"

"It's a bomb," I say, laying it on his desk. "I found it on the railway track."

He jumps up and backs away from his desk, knocking his chair over. "A bomb?" he shouts. "A LIVE BOMB?"

"I think so."

In a few short minutes, bedlam has broken out in this normally quiet little police station. There are constables running in from all directions. And although I don't understand what they are all shouting, I know by the tone of their voices and the looks on their faces that I should get out of there as quick as possible. So I exit the building as fast as I can, with one of the policemen chasing after me. Luckily, I lose him in the surrounding streets.

When I go to bed I can't sleep, worrying about what I did. I worry in case the bomb went off when they were moving it. Will they find out who I am, and where I live? And if they do, and the bomb did go off, what will they do to me? They'll put me in jail forever; I'd never see Mam again.

For the next few days I hope and pray that they don't find out it was me, and it will all die down and come to nothing. And then a few days later, just as I'm thinking it has all died down, I arrive home from school to see a policeman's bike leaning up against the parlor windowsill. I start to tremble all over. I know it is a policeman's bike because of the leather satchel that's hanging from the cross bar.

I make my way round to the back of the house, desperately trying to think of what I'm going to say to the policeman to get me out of this mess.

He might take me away and put me in one of those places for bad boys I've heard about. I know Mrs. Jones won't be on my side; she'll be more than happy to get rid of me, that's a dead cert. I wonder what she is saying to him right now.

I open the scullery door and go into the kitchen and sit down. A few minutes later Mrs. Jones comes into the kitchen. She stands in front of me with her hands on her hips and a menacing look on her face. Then, in a low voice in case the next-door neighbors can hear her, she says, "There's a policeman in the house waiting to see you. You're in very serious trouble. Do you know that? Very serious trouble."

I try my best to look innocent, and tell her that I don't know what she's talking about.

"Don't pretend you don't know," she says. "You know damn well why there's a policeman here. I don't know what I'm going to do with you, bringing policemen to my door. You've never brought anything but trouble since you came here. What will the neighbors think? Never had this with my own children."

She tells me to stay where I am and not to go out until the sergeant is ready to see me. Then she goes back into the parlor where the sergeant is helping himself to a cup of tea and a plate of finely cut sandwiches.

Mrs. Jones is very, very particular about who she allows into her parlor. The fact that this policeman is a sergeant and not an ordinary constable is probably the reason why he isn't eating his sandwiches in the kitchen.

In all the time I lived in that house, the only occasion Frank and I were allowed in the parlor was when old Bryn died. We were so nervous at knocking something over when we entered that each step we took was like a soldier walking through a mine field. And even though that room was rarely used, she never failed to polish and dust everything in there at least three times a week.

I'm sat at the kitchen table scared to the sole of my boots, waiting for the policeman to come in. And the longer I'm sat there, the more worried I get. Then I hear the parlor door open, and the sound of his heavy footsteps as he slowly walks down the lobby. He's so tall that he has to bend his head in the doorway as he enters the kitchen.

He gives me a stern look as he lowers his mighty frame onto the chair next to me. I'm so scared by now, I start to cry.

"Please don't take me away," I blurt out. "I didn't know."

"Didn't know what, Raymond?"

"The bomb—I didn't know you weren't supposed to pick them up."

He unbuttons his top pocket and pulls out his notepad and puts it on the table while he fumbles in his other pocket for his pencil. "Right then," he says. "Let's have your name?"

"Raymond Evans, sir"

"Age?"

"Six and a half, sir."

"School?"

"St. Peter's, sir."

"Do your parents live in Llanelli?"

"My mother does, sir."

"Where's your father?"

"In the Royal Air Force, sir." *Right now I wish I was with him.*

"Been on the railway tracks before?"

"Never, sir, that was the first time."

Mrs. Jones is standing behind him. "He's telling lies, she says. "He's always on the tracks. He's been told a million times about going on the tracks, but he doesn't take any notice."

I shake my head. "I haven't, sir; not until then."

"I think you have Raymond."

"No, sir, honestly, no."

I can tell by the look on his face that he doesn't believe a word I'm saying.

"I don't think you're telling the truth, Raymond," he says. "I think you're always going on the railway lines."

Mrs. Jones butts in again. "He is, he's a liar."

"I'm not a liar, sir. It was the first time, honest. Please don't take me away."

"I don't think it is. A little bird told me a much different story, and it wasn't Mrs. Jones. I think you're always on the railway tracks. You use them for a shortcut from school don't you, Raymond?"

Georgie Mathews, he's told him. I'll bet that's who it was.

All this, of course, is to frighten me, and believe me it is working.

"You could have blown everyone up in the police station, do you realize that?"

"Yes, sir. I'm very sorry. I'll never go near a bomb again."

"Did you know that two little boys about the same age as you were blown up by a bomb recently?"

I had heard about it, because they were all talking about it in school. "No, sir, I didn't."

"They picked it up just like you did, but they weren't so lucky. Six feet down in a coffin, that's where they are now."

"Yes, sir."

"How would you like to be six feet down in a coffin?"

"I wouldn't, sir."

"You will if you go around picking bombs up, won't you?"

"Yes, sir."

"Why did you pick the bomb up, Raymond?"

"I don't know, sir."

"And what about Mrs. Jones here, look at all the worry you're giving her. It's not very fair on her, is it? After all, she was good enough to take you into her nice home, wasn't she?"

I would much prefer to be living on another planet than living in Mrs. Jones' nice home.

"Yes, sir, she was."

"If I give you one more chance, will you promise never to do it again?"

"Yes, sir, I promise. Thank you, sir."

"And never go on the railway tracks again."

"No, sir, I promise. I'll never go on the tracks again."

He stood up, put his helmet on, buttoned his top pocket, thanked Mrs. Jones for the tea and sandwiches, and left. What a relief to hear Mrs. Jones close the door behind him.

She comes back into the kitchen, wags her finger in my face, and shouts at me for bringing a policeman to her door. She says she's so embarrassed by the whole episode that she wouldn't be surprised if her neighbors never speak to her again.

They're Drowning People

In The Church!

Mrs. Jones sends me to Johnson's, the cobbler's, to see if her shoes are ready. She'd called to pick them up a few days prior, but was told that they hadn't even been started on. As usual, she became very annoyed and demanded to know when they would be ready. Because he has such a large backlog, Mr. Johnson tells her it'll be at least another seven days before he would even get to her shoes. Of course that's not good enough for Mrs. Jones, not by a long chalk.

"I'm not waiting another week for my shoes," she says. "I need them for a special occasion."

It's nearly closing time, and Mr. Johnson is tired and in no mood for one of Mrs. Jones' tantrums. "Why is it," he asks, "that every time you bring your shoes in to be mended, they're always needed for a special occasion?

"Well, I never," Mrs. Jones retorts. "I've a good mind to take my business elsewhere."

"Then take them elsewhere," the cobbler says. "I don't care. I've no intention of putting you before my other customers, not now, or any other time"

Mrs. Jones leans over and bangs her fist on the counter. "I've been a customer here for over forty years, surely that's a good enough reason for you to do mine before that pair you're doing."

Mr. Johnson takes her shoes from one of the little pigeon holes, puts them in a brown paper bag, passes them over and politely says, "If you want them repaired that quick, Mrs. Jones, then take them to Station Road. Maybe he can do them for you."

Being too proud to admit that she prefers Mr. Johnson to mend her shoes and not the cobbler on Station Road, Mrs. Jones pushes the shoes back over to the other side of the counter, and with a sarcastic tone in her voice says, "I would, if it wasn't so far to walk."

With that she bursts out of the shop, nearly slamming the door off its hinges.

So when I'm leaving the house this day, I'm given strict instructions that if her shoes aren't ready when I get there, he's to stop what he's doing and do hers instead.

"Here's a note," she says. "I've wrapped it around the money. It's for Mr. Johnson; make sure he reads it."

Mr. Johnson, like his father before him, has always earned his living mending boots and clogs and handbags. Since he was four-teen, as a matter of fact, right out of school.

The faded sign over his shop, which is just barely legible, says, "W. JOHNSON & SON. COBBLERS by TRADE. ESTABLISHED 1865." I asked him one day why he doesn't get a nice, new sign. He walked outside, looked up, and said, "Don't want a new one. My father did that sign himself, many, many years ago. And anyway, I've been here that long; it wouldn't matter if I didn't have a sign, everyone knows where I am."

He reads her note and passes me her shoes over the counter. "She's a bossy bitch, that one," he says. "How the hell Bryn put up with her for so long is beyond me." I pick the bag up and head for the door.

"There's an extra thrupp'ny bit in the change," he shouts as I'm closing the door. "That's for you, so don't mix it up with her change; put it in your other pocket now."

I tuck the shoes under my arm and instead of putting the thrupp'ny bit in my pocket, I stick it in the gap between my two front teeth and walk along twiddling my tongue against it. I've no idea what kind of enjoyment I got out of this, but I was always doing it, especially when I was bored. Like standing for a long time in a queue, for instance.

"It's dirty, you silly boy," Mrs. Jones would say. "You don't know where it's been before you got hold of it, and it'll serve you right if it gets stuck."

I should have taken heed of her warning, because on this particular occasion when I pressed my tongue against the coin to flick it back into my hand, to my horror, it wouldn't come out. It wouldn't even budge. I was so panic stricken, I let her newly mended shoes drop onto the muddy garden soil, took hold of the coin with my fingers, and began to tug. The excruciating pain that followed was too much; I couldn't help it, I gave out such an agonizing cry, I'm sure the people in the next street must have heard it. Our next door neighbor came running out into her garden, looked over the fence and shouted, "Good God what's wrong? What have you done?"

I ignored her and ran into the scullery, shouting at the top of my voice, "Aunthy! Aunthy!" She couldn't hear me, of course, because she was in the parlor. I ran up the lobby and banged on the door as hard as I could. "God in heaven," she shouted, as she opened the door. "What's wrong? What's all the banging for?"

I pointed to the coin in my mouth. "You stupid boy," she screamed. "You frightened the living daylights out of me."

"Pleathe get it out," I begged. "It's hurthing."

"It's your own fault," she said. "It can stay there as far as I'm concerned. I'm not getting it out for you."

"Pleathe, pleathe get it out."

"How many times have I told you not to put coins in your mouth?"

I put my hands together like I was praying. "I'm thorry. Pleathe get it out."

But she wasn't listening, she just pushed me aside and went into the kitchen to look for her shoes. "Where's my shoes? Didn't he have them ready?"

I ran out to the garden, wiped the mud from them with my sleeve, and brought them in. "I suppose I'd better get you to the dentist" she said, after she finished examining them. "Go and put your coat on. You're more trouble than you're worth."

When we arrived at the dentist, Mrs. Jones sent me into the waiting room while she waited to speak to his secretary.

There were about a dozen people in the waiting room, so I didn't bother sitting down; I stood in a corner at the back of the room and covered my mouth with my handkerchief. A few minutes later, a very large lady wearing a white coat came in. She stopped by the door and looked around until she saw me.

"Are you Raymond Evans?"

"Yeth."

She marched over to where I was standing, snatched my hand away from my mouth, and said, "OPEN UP." She stood back with her Popeye arms folded, shook her head slowly from side to side, and said, "So you're the one are you?" "You're the one that sticks coins in between his teeth."

Everyone turned around to have a look. It was very embarrassing. The big, fat nurse led me into a small room and sat me in a chair. I was holding the handkerchief against my mouth again. "Take your hand away from your mouth," she demanded. "How do you expect me to do anything with your hand in the way?"

When I moved my hand, she bent down, looked into my mouth, and before I had a chance to stop her, she grabbed the coin and began tugging at it. And no matter how many times I tried to push her hand away, she held on and wouldn't let go. I howled with pain. "Be quiet," she said. "Everyone can hear you." When she finally got it out, she placed it in my hand, and with a look of sneering gratification on her face, said, "Maybe that will teach you a lesson not to put coins in your mouth next time. Go on, you can go now."

We walked home with the lady whose husband owned the chip shop on the corner of our street. She'd brought her son, Sam, along to have a tooth extracted. We became very good friends after that, right up until the end of the war, as a matter of fact. And although I'd been in Llanelli for the better part of ten months or so, he was the first Welsh boy that chose to ignore his Welsh friends and play with an evacuee such as me. I met up with Sam many years after the war on one of my visits to Llanelli. And it wasn't until then, after all those years, that I found out that he'd been beaten up on more than one occasion just for playing with me.

* * * * *

Even after I left that street to live somewhere else, I still called at his house to walk partway to school together. Sam attended a private school, where all the boys wore green uniforms and carried their books in leather satchels. One day he opened his satchel, took out his books, and showed me all the many things he had to learn. I was glad I didn't have to go to his school. I liked Sam a lot. He didn't show off just because his parents owned their own business and he attended a private school.

The first morning I knocked on Sam's door to go to school, his mother invited me in to wait because Sam hadn't quite finished his breakfast. Her husband, who was sat in front of the fire toasting bread, asked me if I'd like a cup of tea and a piece of toast. Always hungry, I didn't refuse. When I'd eaten it, which was rather quickly, Sam's mother asked me if I'd like another piece. But before I had a chance to take it from the plate, her husband said, "You'll have to sing us a song first." I pulled my hand away and looked at him, puzzled as to why he would want me to sing a song.

"I can't sing," I said, "and I don't know any songs."

"You can," he said. "I was listening to you the other day when you were playing outside my window."

I pretended that I didn't know what he was talking about. "Don't remember that," I said, "must've been someone else."

"It was you alright," he said. "You were singing that song, "You Are My Woodbine.""

I shook my head. "Wasn't me," I said, "it was one of the other boys."

"It was you alright," he said. "I was watching you."

His silly little game was beginning to annoy me; it was making me feel like I was begging for food. "But I'm no good at singing," I said, hoping that would be the end of the matter. "I don't have a good voice."

"Doesn't matter," he said. "Just sing it boy; you can have another piece of toast then. Surely you must sing in chapel, Raymond, just pretend you're in chapel."

"I don't sing in chapel." "You don't?"

"No, I don't. Everyone sings in Welsh in the chapel, and I don't know how to sing in Welsh."

His wife told him to stop teasing me and give me the toast. "Just a few words, Raymond," he said, "that's all; then you can have your toast." The temptation of another piece of toast was too much, so with scarlet cheeks, I started to sing. It was the only song I knew. Where it originated from I've no idea, but in those days, all the kids used to sing it. It was sung to the tune of "You Are My Sunshine." The words won't make a lot of sense to you, they didn't to me, but it went like this,

> You are my Woodbine, my double Woodbine
> My box of matches, my pint of beer
> My double whisky to make me frisky
> So please don't take my Woodbine away.

Crazy, isn't it? Never made the top ten. A Woodbine, by the way, is a cigarette (sometimes called a "Woodie"), which could be purchased in packets of five or ten. If you wanted a packet of ten, you asked for a "Double Woodbine." Whether you can still buy them, I'm not sure. I know I've not seen them over here in America.

* * * * *

It may interest you to know that the Welsh language was spoken by as much as 90% of the population in those days, in the homes, in the schools, and, of course, in chapel. And chapel was a place I was required to visit at least twice every Sunday. On some occasions, even three times. The reason why? Mrs. Jones required a minimum of at least two church services each Sunday to keep her soul in sound repair.

Chapel for a seven year old who couldn't speak, never mind sing a word of the Welsh language, was, I have to say, a terribly boring place to spend a Sunday. Whenever I complained about going to church she'd say, "Men who want to make anything of themselves must go to chapel; always remember that."

And she was always nudging me with her elbow during hymn singing; it was really annoying. "Come on, Raymond, stand up and sing."

I'd shake my head. "Can't Mrs. Jones, can't sing in Welsh."

"Just try and read the words from the hymn book, surely you can do that. People are staring at you; it's very embarrassing for me."

I tried to read the words, but it was impossible; it looked like
Dutch and German all mixed up.

One Sunday, when the service had finished and everyone was shuffling their way along the aisle to shake hands with the vicar on their way out, the man who took the collection that particular day comes scurrying up behind and grabs me by my collar.

"I'm up to your little game, sonny," he says. "I saw you what you did."

"What game?" I ask, trying to pull his hand away.

"Tapping the collection plate and pretending you've put your money on it. That's not a nice thing to do is it? Especially in God's house."

Everyone stops and starts to form a circle around the collection man and me.

"What's going on?" Mrs. Jones asks. "What's he done?" "It's in his pocket."

"I'm sorry," Mrs. Jones says. "Can't hear you. What was it you said?"

"It's in his pocket," he shouts. "The penny; he's kept it." "In his pocket? What's in his pocket?"

"The penny," the man says, still holding on to my collar. "He put his collection money in his pocket instead of putting it on the plate. I saw him do it."

"Is this true, Raymond?" Mrs. Jones asks. "Did you keep the penny?"

"No," I say. "I put it on the plate."\

"He's lying," the man says. "I saw him do it. It's in his pocket. Search him."

By this time, the circle of people around me has doubled, and they are all watching my very embarrassed landlady go through my trouser and jacket pockets. When she doesn't find anything, she immediately demands an apology from my accuser for embarrassing her (not for embarrassing me), and suggests to the vicar, who's burst through the crowd to see what's going on, that in future he should give the collection job to someone else.

"I'm not apologizing to anyone," the collection man says. "I know he's got the penny on him somewhere, where I don't know, but it's on him somewhere."

"Well, I never!" Mrs. Jones says. "Are you calling me a liar? You've just seen me search him."

"No, I'm not. I'd just like to search him myself, that's

all." "Then go on, search him if it makes you feel happy."

He kneels down in front of me and proceeds to go through my pockets. And when he doesn't find anything, he searches me again, pulling the lining out of my pockets in frustration. He shakes his head.

"I was certain he didn't put that penny on the plate. I'd have bet my life on it."

"Well, what about that apology?" Mrs. Jones demands. "I'm entitled to an apology, especially in front of all these people."

"Just a minute," the man says, bending down again, "there's one place we haven't looked."

He pulls my socks down. The gloating expression on his face when he sees the penny pop out can only be described as that of a man that's just solved the crime of the century. Holding the coin between two fingers, he stands up, stretches his hand to the ceiling for all to see and shouts, "I knew it! I told you so! I knew he had it." There's a loud chorus of gasps as "Sherlock Holmes" shows the penny to the vicar.

"He was trying to steal money from the collection plate vicar."

"Is that what you were doing, boy," the vicar asks, "trying to steal money from the collection plate?"

"No, sir, I wasn't."

Mrs. Jones taps the vicar on the shoulder. "I'm sorry about this vicar," she says. " I didn't see him do it. It's very embarrassing."

"Oh, I see," the vicar says. "He's staying with you is he, Mrs. Jones?"

Mrs. Jones doesn't have time to answer because "Sherlock Holmes" butts in. "Yes, that's right vicar. He's one of those evacuees from up north. Liverpool, I think, by the sound of his accent."

"Don't worry about it, Mrs. Jones," the vicar says, taking hold of my hand. "I'll sort it out."

He leads me into the vestry.

"Shall I come as well, vicar?" "Sherlock Holmes"

asks. "No, thank you," he says. "I'll sort it out."

The vicar sits me down and then turns the chair to face a stained glass picture of Jesus on the cross. "Now, before we start," he says, "you see who's looking down on you, don't you?"

"Yes, sir."

"Do you know who he is?"

"Jesus, sir."

"That's right, it's Jesus, which means you have to tell the truth when I ask you a question. No fibs, OK? Not in front of him."

"OK."

"Right then, why did you steal the penny from the collection plate?"

"I didn't steal it, it was my penny *(well, Mrs. Jones' really)*. I
just pretended to put it on the plate."

"Well, that's the same as stealing you see Raymond. When you came here today, you did intend to give your penny to the church, didn't you Raymond?"

"Yes, sir."

"But you didn't give to the church, did you? Why did you change your mind?"

"I wanted to buy a penny bag of broken biscuits with it because I'm hungry."

"Oh, I see, a penny bag of broken biscuits. Mmmm ... so that's why you kept the penny, is it?"

"Yes."

"Not a very good excuse I'm afraid, Raymond"

"I was hungry. If I wasn't so hungry, I wouldn't have kept it." "Have you done it before?"

I'll have to tell him the truth, otherwise I could go to hell instead of heaven.

"Yes, just once."

"Don't you get enough to eat then?"

I squeeze my lips together and shrug my shoulders.

"I'll tell you what," the vicar says. "I will give you another penny to buy some biscuits, but you must promise me you'll never do it again, never take money from the plate."

"I promise, I won't do it again."

"And anytime you want a penny for a bag of broken biscuits, you come and see me."

I thank him for the penny and put it in my pocket.

Being that the conversation was in Welsh, I don't know what he said to Mrs. Jones when we came out of the vestry, but whatever it was, considering the circumstances, she was very lenient with me that day; I wasn't even sent to bed early.

* * * * *

It's another Sunday and we're getting ready to go to church. But because we have a few minutes to spare, and for reasons better known to her, she decided to give me some lessons in "manhood."

I'm sitting at the kitchen table, trying to look interested while she stands in the middle of the floor, instructing me on how a gentleman should walk with a lady. "A gentleman," she says, "must always walk on the outside of the pavement, never on the inside."

"Why," I ask, trying to give the impression of being interested.

"Because it puts the lady further away from the horses, that's why. You must have seen Mr. Jones do that when we were walking to church every Sunday, didn't you?"

I say yes, but can't really remember.

"Well, now that I've told you, just remember it in the future. You must always walk on the outside when we are going to church."

"Yes."

Thinking she's finished, I get up to get my cap and coat from the back of the kitchen door, but I've hardly moved when she grabs my arm and pulls me back.

"I'm not finished yet," she snaps. "Sit down."

I'm not in any mood to be listening to any of her lessons in manhood, especially on a Sunday morning when I'm about to leave for chapel. But she continues to jabber on, so I switch off and let it all go in one ear and out of the other. And as I lean on the table watching her mouth going ten to the dozen, I imagine myself getting up from my chair, going straight up to her, face-to-face, and telling her that I'm very sorry, but from today I'm putting my foot down.

What do you mean she'll say, how dare you talk to me like that. Then I'll say, "Now listen to me Mrs. Jones, I've as much

interest in becoming a gentleman as Adolph Hitler has in losing
the war. And as regards going to church every single Sunday, well,
it's like this. I don't want to go to church. I don't like going to
church. Neither today nor any other day, come to mention it. You
go on your own Mrs. Jones, and I'll read a comic or play in the
street with the other kids."

"Are you listening to me?"

"Oh, I'm sorry, Mrs. Jones, I was miles away."

"As I was saying, today, when we get to the church, instead
of barging in front like you always do, you must stand to one side
and open the door for me, just like a gentleman would."

"Yes, Mrs. Jones, I won't forget."

But I did forget, and I barged in front of her and got another
lecture when we sat down.

The other thing I hate about going to church is having to
kneel on a piece of coconut matting when saying prayers; talk
about torture. It wouldn't be so bad if I were in long pants, but
I'm not, I'm still in short ones. I've complained to Mrs. Jones
about it, asking her if I can stand up during prayers. "Stand up,"
she says, with a look of disgust on her face. "Stand up during
prayers? Of course you can't stand up during prayers."

"Well, what about me getting one of those cushions that you
kneel on then?"

"You can't have a cushion, they're only for the likes of us
older people. Now be quiet and don't be such a baby."

"Can I rest my knees on my hands then?"

"No, you can't. How can you when you're praying?"

I put my hands together and pray, but I don't say the same
prayers that everyone one else is saying. I ask God to rush the vicar

through the prayers as fast as he can. I tell him it's not fair that I should have to kneel on coconut matting when others have nice soft cushions to kneel on. I tell him the coconut matting is not only very painful to kneel on, but it also makes deep holes in my skin. So deep in fact, they are still there even when I get home.

The morning service starts at eleven o'clock, but we have to leave the house at ten, even though the church is only five minutes down the road. Why? Just because she doesn't want anyone else taking her usual place in the balcony. Every Sunday it's the same old thing, the two of us sitting up there entirely on our own when most of the congregation are probably still fast asleep in bed. We sit there twiddling our thumbs in the two end seats of the third row, not the second row or the first row, it has to be the two end seats of the third row. I don't know why she even chooses to sit up in the balcony. It's so high up, I'm sure it's impossible for her to hear what's going on anyway. In fact, the vicar has to literally shout at the top of his voice just so the rest of the gallery can hear him. But then thinking about it, I don't suppose it really matters as far as my landlady is concerned; even if they sat her next to the altar, she probably still wouldn't hear anything. Of course, it doesn't bother me where we sit; the entire service is spoken and sung in Welsh anyway.

And the part I dread most about the whole service is the sermon. I wish the vicar would at least speak it in English. Then it wouldn't be so monotonously boring. When I first came to the church he frightened the living daylights out of me. He's so demonstrative and volatile when he's giving his sermons I thought he was telling everybody off. But he doesn't frighten me anymore, not like that first time. In fact, I was so frightened by his behavior that first day, whenever he'd look up to the balcony in my direction, I'd slide down in my seat so he couldn't see me.

* * * * *

In front of the altar is a stage, and below the stage is what looks to me to be a swimming pool.

My recollection of the first total immersion baptism I witnessed is as clear today as it was then. I'm sitting there, gazing up at the ceiling, when four ladies dressed in long white gowns suddenly appear from behind the organ and line up alongside the "swimming pool." I've never seen a baptism before, so I have no idea why these ladies would want to take a swim during a church service, especially in a long white gown instead of a bathing costume. I spring up out of my seat to get a better look.

Mrs. Jones grabs my arm and pulls me back down. "Sit down and be still," she whispers firmly in my ear.

I sit for a few minutes, extremely inquisitive as to what was going on, until eventually I can't wait any longer. I touch her on her shoulder to get her attention, and in my best professional sign language, point a finger toward the swimming pool in a "what's going on gesture." She nearly touches my nose with hers and says, "Shhhhh. Be QUIET and don't POINT."

I'm determined to see what's happening, so before she has a chance to stop me, I jump up and run down to the front of the balcony. Now I've got a full view of everything. She's livid, but far too embarrassed to come after me.

When the vicar dunks the first one under the water, which appears to be done against the young lady's will, I stand wide eyed and open mouthed, unable to take in what I'm really seeing. And the dunking isn't just for a brief second or two; her head is held down for so long, I truly think he's trying to drown her. When he gets to the last one I notice that she's much younger than the others, only about eleven or twelve. Surely, I say to myself, he's not going to keep her under for the same length of time as the others, but he does the cruel thing; he doesn't care. When he finishes dunking her, he leads them away, back into a room behind the organ. They look like drowned rats. That's when I return to my seat. Mrs. Jones is fuming. "Just wait until we get home," she says in a low voice.

The conversation on the way home between Mrs. Jones and some of her church-going friends is about my behavior in church. Even though they are speaking in Welsh, it's easy to tell it's about me as they keep looking down, shaking their heads and tutting. But I don't care. As long as they are not planning to have me dunked in that swimming pool next Sunday, they can say what they like.

When we get into the house, I'm given a severe telling off. "The whole street's talking about you; do you know that? What do you think you were doing? Running down the aisle like that. I've never been so embarrassed in my entire life."

(How many times have I heard that?)

"I'm sorry," I say. "I won't do it again."

"Sorry? Sorry? It's too late now to be sorry. They were getting baptized, that's all it was. Do you understand? BAPTIZED." She stares up at the ceiling, blows a long sigh, and says, "It'd better not happen again, because you won't get off so lightly the next time, I can promise you that."

Having no intentions of becoming a member of the congregation and being drowned on stage, I tell her that I don't want to go to that church anymore. "He's not going to dunk me under any water." Lost for words, she gives me a disgusted look and stomps out of the kitchen.

No matter how much I'm threatened, I refuse to go back to that church; at least for the next couple of weeks anyway. "I'll go to Sunday school," I tell her, "but I'm not going back to that church to get drowned on stage."

A Gas Mask Drill for Young Children at School

Young Evacuee on Train
A very young boy, thumb in mouth, sits aboard a train waiting to
be evacuated to the English countryside. Many young children were
evacuated from British cities to rural locations in hopes they would
escape German air raids. 1942

Children Kneel under desks during Air Raid Drill A school in southern England performs an air raid drill in response to German bombing raids in the area.

Christmas in an Air Raid Shelter
A young girl sleeps under Christmas decorations and stockings stuffed with treats in 1940. Santa Claus has visited this British home, but World War II means Christmas must be celebrated in a bomb shelter.

Carrying Child from Bombed Home
A rescue worker carries a toddler to safety after her home was
damaged in an air raid.

Mrs. Williams children with their pet rabbit

Mr. & Mrs. Williams

**My sisters Muriel & Elsie with their
wartime foster mother**

Air Raids And The All Clear

During the early months of 1940, people in my hometown had given up believing there was ever going to be a war. And I don't suppose you could blame them really, not when you consider that up until then there hadn't been one single bomb dropped on Liverpool. In fact no one was even looking for German planes in the skies anymore. Parents who had sent their children to safer places began to have second thoughts; they wanted them back in their own homes. The trickle soon turned into thousands.

But the trouble was, those that did return found that their schools had been commandeered by the military, the fire service, and, in some cases, for the storage of emergency food. Since compulsory education had been abandoned at the beginning of the war, it was a trying time for the authorities, to say the least.

Furthermore, for the evacuees who decided to return to Liverpool (including a school friend of mine), the decision would turn out to be a mistake, one that would eventually cost them their lives.

The allied forces during this time were being forced back by a very powerful advancing German army; things were now getting very serious. So serious, in fact, that Winston Churchill (who was now the Prime Minister) was prompted to declare to the House of Commons, "We are in the preliminary stages of one of the greatest battles in history. I have nothing to offer but blood, toil, tears, and sweat" (May 13, 1940, House of Commons).

And in a later broadcast he gave another warning to the people, "There will be many men, and many women, in this island who, when the ordeal comes upon them, as come it will, will feel comfort, and even pride, that they are sharing the perils of our lads at the front." And around the same time, the most famous of all his speeches was given. "We shall fight on the beaches, we shall fight on the hills, we shall never surrender."

* * * * *

March of that year, according to records, was when Llanelli experienced her first bombing. And what's interesting to note is that the exact spot where one of the bombs landed is now a sand bunker on one of Llanelli's newest golf courses. But the most vivid recollection I have of a bombing raid took place one evening in the following July 1940.

About eight-thirty in the evening I was sound asleep in bed, when suddenly I was awakened by the loud wailing sound of the air raid sirens. I sat bolt upright in bed, trembling and wondering what was happening. It was a loud, penetrating sound that seemed to get right inside your head and body. In fact, many years after the war the sound of those sirens that the factories decided to use to call their workers in always gave me goose pimples.

Suddenly old Bryn rushed in with a couple of blankets under his arm, threw one over me, picked me up, and dashed down the stairs to the air raid shelter in the garden. By the time we arrived there his chest was wheezing so badly I thought he was going to collapse at any moment. He tucked me in between the sheets on the top bunk and told me not to be frightened, that we would be safe in the air raid shelter.

I lay listening to all sorts of commotion coming from the neighbors next door, scurrying into their little hole in the ground. On her way out of the kitchen Mrs. Jones had grabbed the rest of the blankets, the gas masks, and the emergency box. She had a special place for them in a cupboard behind the door. (I think everyone had an emergency box; they were essential for the long nights in the air raid shelter.) She was already laying on her bunk when Bryn and I got there, the blankets pulled tightly over her head. The sirens stopped after a few minutes and we waited in silence listening for the German airplanes. Then, after a few more minutes, we heard what was to become the all too familiar droning sound of the German bombers as they got nearer and nearer. Bryn was standing in the doorway looking up to the night sky. "Here they come," he said. "I can just see them in the distance. There must be hundreds of the buggers." Although I could feel my heart thumping with fear, I couldn't resist getting down from my bunk and poking my head outside to see the planes. I could hear Mrs. Jones praying and crying at the same time.

The sight of those planes has stuck in my memory to this day. Wave after wave of enemy bombers swept across the moonlit sky gradually dropping lower and lower until I thought they were going to land in the streets around us. And the noise from their engines was so unbearably loud that I thought my ears were going to burst. I don't know how many planes were in the sky that night, but I'm sure there must have been hundreds of them. When the last few planes passed over and disappeared into the distance, Bryn tucked me up in my bunk. "I've never seen so many planes," he said. "Swansea's really going to get it tonight, poor devils." It was very cold in the shelter, so he threw a blanket over his shoulders and told Mrs. Jones he was going to make a cup of cocoa for us all. As he walked back to the house he stopped and looked up to the sky. "That bloody Adolph Hitler," he shouted. "He'll get his comeuppance one day; our lads will see to that."

Bearing in mind that the city of Swansea was twelve miles away, the noise from the explosions was sometimes so loud that it sounded like the bombs were landing in the next street. It was starting to break light when the bombings finally stopped. I wanted to get back into the house out of the cold and dampness of the air raid shelter. The tiny bit of heat that came from the paraffin heater not only made the air stale, but also drenched the walls with condensation. I listened impatiently for the "all clear" to sound. "We can't leave yet," Bryn said. "The all clear won't sound until every "Gerry" has crossed back over the channel." He sat on his bunk to listen to the wireless.

About twenty minutes had passed when suddenly there was an ear piercing whistling noise, followed by a few seconds of silence, then an almighty explosion. It shook the air raid shelter so badly that I thought it was about to collapse around us. Clouds of dust floated down from the metal ceiling above making it impossible to breathe properly. I was curled up under the blankets, my hands pressed against my ears. That night I really thought I was going to die. Bryn shot up from his bunk to see if the house had been bombed; amazingly it was still standing. He looked up to the sky to see a lonely bomber disappearing into the distance. And as its droning sound became fainter and fainter he put his head inside the shelter and said, "I think that's it. That's the last of them. The all clear will sound shortly." The bomb had actually landed on a shop in the next street. Shortly after that the all clear finally sounded, and what a lovely sound that was.

As we emerged from the shelter and made our way back into

the house, I could hear the fire brigade bells ringing as they raced toward the bombed shop. I went straight to bed; I didn't have to go to school that day.

* * * * *

My landlady spent most evenings in the parlor, either listening to the wireless, pedaling her sewing machine, or sleeping in her chair. She had no desire to be in my company; the longest conversation we had was when she was sending me on a message. Of course, she never wanted to take in an evacuee in the first place, as she repeatedly told me. "It was Mr. Jones who contacted the billeting officer to bring you here, not me," she would always remind me.

The nights when it was raining, preventing me from playing out in the street, I spent in the kitchen alone, either listening to the wireless, or reading my favorite comics, the "Dandy," the "Beano," and the "Film Fun." I got the money to purchase them by running messages for a couple of the neighbors, or taking the odd bottle back to the shop and getting the deposit on it. The only other times she spoke to me was when she gave me my meals. I was so desperate to leave and find a new billet that I asked a friend on our way home from school one day to ask his mother if she would take me in. "Its just for a while," I told him (hoping of course she might let me stay until the war was over), "until Mrs. Davis, our billeting officer, finds me a new billet." He thought it was a great idea so he agreed to ask her. I waited outside with my fingers crossed, not just on one hand, but on both, but it didn't do any good. She came out and told me she couldn't because of her full-time job in one of the factories. "I'm sorry," she said, "it takes me all my time just looking after my own son."

Somehow Mrs. Jones found out and, in her temper, contacted

Mrs. Davis the same day and told her she wanted me out of her house as soon as possible.

The following Sunday my mother came to the house to find out why I hadn't been to see her, and what I'd done to provoke my landlady into getting me moved. I think Mrs. Davis must have been to see her. As far as visiting her, I lied and told her it was too far to walk. The truth was that whenever I did visit my mother, I never wanted to leave. So I just thought it better to stay away.

Mrs. Jones and Mam were in the parlor talking while I sat in the kitchen. When Mam came out, Mrs. Jones stayed in the parlor to give Mam and I a few minutes on our own. Mam sat down, put her arms around me, and in a whisper said she would ask Mrs. Davis to find me a new billet as soon as possible.

"You must understand that I can't take you in with me; there's just not enough room." Her eyes shone with unshed tears as she struggled to explain how impossible it was for her to take me with her. "The war can't go on forever, then we'll all be back together again, Dad as well. I promise."

Runaway Ray

The summer turns into winter, the long cold nights dragging slowly by. Mrs. Davis keeps promising to move me next week, but next week never comes.

January 1941 … still no new billet. Mrs. Jones keeps asking me if Mrs. Davis has mentioned anything. I tell her she hasn't. Disappointed, she goes out mumbling and shaking her head like she always does. I think she hates me even more than when I first arrived here. I can't take it anymore, so before I go to sleep tonight I'll pack my things in my haversack, hide it under the bed, and run away tomorrow. Then they'll have to find me a new place.

Sometime during the night I'm suddenly awakened by the unmistakable droning of German aircraft. Unmistakable because during the preceding few weeks, like everyone else, I've learned to tell the difference between the engine noises of our own aircraft and those of the German ones. And because the planes are flying so low, I take a peek through a little opening in the curtains so I can see them. The sky's full of them, and I know where they're going

... Swansea again. I get back into bed and I pull the sheets over my head and put my hands over my ears so that I can't hear the bombs dropping. But surprisingly enough the raid only lasts a short time before everything falls back into silence again.

It's still dark when I awake the next morning, but because I don't have a clock in my room, I go down into the kitchen to see the time. Although it's still very early, I think it's too risky to go back to bed in case I don't wake up in time. So I creep back to my bedroom, get dressed, sling my haversack and gas mask over my shoulder, and tiptoe out through the scullery onto the lane and into the moonlight.

It's a full moon, high and bright. The streets are dark, empty, and silent. It's so quiet that I walk very slowly past the houses in case the studs in my boots wake anyone up. When I get near the ARP building, I cross over the road so that the warden doesn't hear me going past. He's bound to wonder why a young boy like me is out so early. As I hurry along, I look up at the big, silvery barrage balloons floating silently in the sky. Maybe it's my imagination, but they seem much lower than normal, especially the one that's right above me. I've never seen one so low; maybe it's come loose and no one knows about it. One broke away by Eddie's house a few weeks ago and tore down most of the chimney pots in their street. I run faster to get away from it.

The school isn't far away and it only takes me about fifteen minutes to get there. Problem is, I have at least two hours to wait before one of the teachers arrives to open up. I crouch down inside the passageway of the vestry and sit on my haversack.

It's a typical cold, frosty January morning and I start to shiver uncontrollably, cursing myself for leaving my raincoat on the back of the kitchen door. I'm tempted to go back for it, but Mrs. Jones is bound to be up when I get there as she's always up at the crack of dawn to start her cleaning. She's certainly not the type of person that enjoys a sleep in now and again—that would certainly mess her schedule up.

Trying to take my mind off the cold, I begin to think back to the times before the war, when we were all together. I wonder whether the nice house on Brookbridge Road has been bombed, or will it still be there after the war. Would I ever see my Dad again, or would he be killed like so many of my friends' dads. Then I start to wonder what my new foster parents will be like. Maybe I'd be lucky enough to get a billet like Albert's. He's still with the same lady who took him in when we first arrived in South Wales. He loves his billet, lucky thing. And here I am, on my way to my third already. In fact, he stayed there right up to the end of the war. Albert's landlady loved him so much that she asked Mam on several occasions if she would allow her to adopt him. Of course Mam refused, but his landlady never gave up trying to change her mind, right up to the very day we were boarding the train to go back to Liverpool, as a matter of fact. I remember us all watching her through the window of the train, pleading with Mam. We all felt sorry for her that day, watching her hug Albert the way she did. She made him promise to come back and visit her.

Albert and George had only been in their new billet for a few short days when their landlady took them out to buy Albert some new school clothes and George a new pair of boots. George didn't need any school clothes because he was leaving school shortly to get a job. In fact, he wasn't in that billet long before he went to live with Mam in her billet. Albert and I were playing on the swings one day when he said to me, "My landlady has bought me a new pair of gray pants, socks, a white shirt, a blazer, and a cap for when I go to school." And if that wasn't enough to make a person envious, he added, "She's even sewn the school badge on the pocket of my blazer and one on the cap."

I would have given anything for a cap with a badge on. It wouldn't have mattered what kind, as long as it was a badge. After he refused to switch caps with me, I asked him if he would ask his landlady to sew a badge on my cap. He said, "You have to belong to a proper school like I do to get a badge; they don't have badges where you are."

"How do you know that?" I snapped back. "Ours is a proper school, just like yours."

"No, it's not," he said. "Your school is a church vestry school; church vestries are not proper schools, so they don't have school badges."

It was about eight-thirty when Miss Grainger arrived. She leaned her bike against the wall and walked over to the vestry door. It wasn't until she stepped into the passageway to unlock the door that she saw me crouched in the corner.

"What are you doing down there?" she asks with a startled look on her face.

"I've ran away from my billet, miss. I want Mrs. Davis to find me a new one."

"And how long have you been waiting there?" "About two hours I think."

"I hope you have a good reason for running away," she says, "because if you haven't, Mrs. Davis will be very annoyed with you. Do you have a good reason for running away Raymond?"

"Yes, miss." "What is it?"

"Mrs. Jones doesn't like me, miss. She doesn't like any evacuees."

"What makes you say that?"

"She told me she doesn't like evacuees, miss. She said it was

Mr. Jones' idea to take us in, not hers."

Miss Grainger makes me a hot cup of cocoa and tells me to sit in front of the fire until the nine o'clock bell.

Mrs. Davis arrives at her usual time of 9:30 and calls me into Miss Grainger's office. I can tell by the expression on her face that I'm in for a good telling off. "Now listen to me young man, you do not run away from your billet just because you don't like it. Do you understand?"

"Yes, Mrs. Davis"

"If you have any complaints about your billet, you should report them to me first. That's why I'm here every morning, to find out if any of you have any complaints. And because of the difficulty of finding you a new billet at such short notice, you'll just have to go back to Mrs. Jones until I do."

"But Mrs. Jones doesn't want me there anymore. She doesn't like evacuees."

"We'll see about that," she says. "I'm sure she'll take you back if I ask her. Go back to your desk. I'll be back before the four o'clock bell."

I know what's going to happen when Mrs. Davis gets there; Mrs. Jones will open the front door just wide enough to poke her nose out, and will tell Mrs. Davis that she doesn't want me back and that she's glad to see the back of me.

When the twelve o'clock bell rings, Miss Grainger tells me to stay behind at my desk. She goes out to the kitchen and brings back a cup of tea and a sandwich for me. It makes me feel very guilty because a person that gives someone half her lunch can't be that bad of person, I say to myself; I'll never call her a bad name again.

It's time for the monitor to ring the four o'clock bell. Mrs. Davis still isn't back. I start to worry whether she's found me a new billet or not. If she hasn't found me one, what's going to happen to me tonight? Where will I sleep? I hope they don't put me in that hostel I've heard so much about, it's full of evacuees that are so misbehaved the billeting officer has an impossible job trying to get them billets. And not only that, most of them are crawling with lice and scabies anyway, and I don't want to catch anything like that, especially scabies. I'd rather go back to Mrs. Jones' any day than catch scabies.

At this point in my young life I began to feel an even deeper sense of insecurity, which later developed into an inferiority complex. And because I was an evacuee, I began to feel that every-one in Llanelli hated me. I'd even stopped visiting my mother because her landlady (the first landlady she stayed with for a short while), for some reason, wouldn't let me in when I arrived there one day. She told me to stay away, and I did for a long time, until Mam moved across the lane into another billet. They were really nice people and Mam liked them a lot. In fact a friendship was formed between Mam and her new landlady that kept them in touch until long after the war, until they died as a matter of fact.

I felt I'd become a nuisance and an intruder on other people's lives. Every time a meal was put down to me, it made me feel like I was a beggar. And even though a year had gone by, I still wasn't fully aware of the enormity and gravity of the situation; what was really going on in the rest of the world. I knew our soldiers were fighting other soldiers, but for what reason, I had no idea. As far as I was concerned, whatever their reason for fighting it was no reason why I should be taken away from my mother and made to live with strangers that didn't want me in their homes. I wanted to go home again, back to Liverpool with all the family, back in our nice new house on Brookbridge Road.

When Mrs. Davis arrived back at the school that day and walked into the classroom, my stomach started to quiver like there was a hundred butterflies inside. After waiting all day, the time had finally come as to what was going to happen to me. Was I about to be taken back to Mrs. Jones' or to a new billet? If she's found me a new billet, are my new foster parents taking me in just because they feel obliged to, or am I going to be lucky enough to move in with someone who really wants me? Please God, make them like me.

Mrs. Davis, still very angry with me for running away from my last billet, takes a firm hold of my hand. "Come on Raymond, I've found you a new billet. We have to hurry. I haven't got all day, I do have other children to see to as well as you."

I pull my hand away from hers and ask if she knows whether the new people I am to stay with really do like evacuees.

"Of course," she says. "They wouldn't take you in otherwise."

I don't believe her. I think they are taking me in because they think they are obligated to. "What if they are like Mrs. Jones?"

"Put your coat on," she scowls. "I'm not arguing with you all day."

"Why don't you ask my mother to take me in with her? I'm sure she'll find room for just one more if you ask her."

"I've told you before, there's no spare room for you in that house, especially now she has a new baby. You must try to settle down and not keep asking to go back to your mother. Now pick up your things, I'm in a hurry."

With my haversack slung over one shoulder, and my gas mask over the other, I follow her out of the classroom.

We've been walking for at least an hour, up one street and down another. I ask her if she's lost her way.

"The house is somewhere around here," she says. "It's just that it's getting too dark to see the street names properly."

I'm beginning to struggle behind because my legs are getting tired, so I try to pull my hand away from hers. She stops and gives me a proper roasting in the middle of the street, and tells me it's all my fault for running away from Mrs. Jones. I tell her she would have run away from Mrs. Jones as well if she lived with her. She waves her finger in my face and tells me not to be cheeky, and to be grateful she was able to find me another billet so soon. Under my breath I tell her if it's anything like the last one, I'll run away again. We walk a bit further and then, with a loud sigh of relief, she says, "This is it, this is the road. The house is just a little further down on the next block, number twenty-six."

She counts down until she arrives at what should be number twenty-six. It's too dark to see the number on the door, so to make sure she's got the right one, she opens the gate and walks up the path to get a closer look. The dilapidated house is to all appearances uninhabited. There are no proper curtains on any of the windows, just black sheets hanging down. I can also see a big hole in the front door where a pane of glass used to be. And the front lawn has enough junk on it that it could easily be mistaken for the local dump.

I stop at the gate and shout, "I don't think this is the right house, Mrs. Davis. It doesn't look like anyone lives here."

When she gets to the door she stands on tiptoes and peers up at the number. "It is the right house; this is your new billet."

I'm speechless; I can't believe what I'm hearing.

"Come on," she shouts impatiently, "don't just stand there."

I shake my head and tell her I don't want to live here. She runs up the path and grabs my arm, "This is your new home," she snaps, "and this is where you will stay. Don't you dare think of running away this time."

She takes her hanky from her pocket and wipes the tears from my eyes, then knocks on the door.

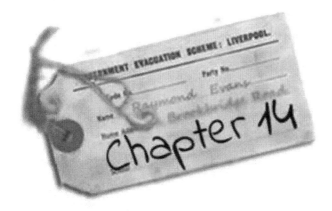

Out Of The Frying Pan

Into The Fire

He's knocked on the door at least four times without an answer, so she shouts through the letter box, "Is there anybody home?" Finally the door opens very slowly. A scruffy boy about my size and age appears. He's got a snotty nose and dirty blonde hair sticking up all over the place.

Mrs. Davis asks if his mother is in. He doesn't answer, just keeps frowning and staring at me. *He looks a bit doolally, I say to myself.* She asks him again, "Is your mother in, sonny?"

He still stares at me, but this time he nods a yes. Mrs. Davis gets very impatient and demands he call his mother right away. Without taking his eyes off me, he shouts, "Maaam, I think it's him, the ev-evacuee."

His mother comes rushing up the lobby, wiping her hands on her pinafore. She gives Scruffy a clip over his ear for not inviting us in. She's tall and gangly, about fifty years of age. She's wearing a very dirty crossover apron, and she's got the biggest hatchet-shaped nose I've ever seen in my life. She reminds me of a witch I've recently seen on a pantomime poster.

"I'm sorry," she says. "I'm in the middle of cooking dinner. Please come in."

A strong musty smell greets us as we're led along a dark hallway into the kitchen. It's a smell that's mixed with cat pee and boiling cabbage.

Mrs. Davis thanks my landlady for taking me in, and says she'll call round in a few weeks to make sure I've settled in. She then turns to me and tells me to be a good boy and to do as I'm told. When she sees the look on my face, she bends down and whispers in my ear, "Remember Raymond, no running away this time. Do you hear me?"

I nod in agreement, but I think she knows I don't mean it.

My landlady closes the door behind her and goes back into the kitchen to carry on with her cooking. I listen to Mrs. Davis' fading footsteps as she walks up the path. I want to open the door and shout after her, *"I hate you Mrs. Davis for leaving me here. I hate everyone."*

Scruffy, who suffers with a bad stammer, wants to know why I'm crying. His mother tells him to mind his own business and to show me where to hang my things. He points to a little door that leads under the stairs. "Hang your stuff in there," he says, "and watch you don't fr-fr-frighten my kittens."

I open the little door and stoop down to reach the coat hooks. The smell that comes out is so strong, I feel like being sick. The hooks are piled high with so many coats that I can't find any room for mine. "Just hang 'em on top of the others," Scruffy says, "and hurry up before the k-k-kittens get out."

I try, but it's too late—the kittens have already scrambled out of the box and onto the floor in the hallway. His mother stops what's she's doing in the kitchen and charges into the hallway cursing and swearing. She scoops them all up with her hands, ducks under the stairs, and chucks them back into the box. Then before she kicks the door shut, she snatches my coat and gas mask out of my hands, stoops down, and throws them on the floor beside the kittens. "Get rid of those bloody cats," she tells Scruffy. "I don't care how you do it, just get rid of them." Scruffy starts crying.

I follow her into the kitchen and sit down while she goes over to see to the pots on the stove.

"You can either call me Mrs. Simmons or Auntie," she shouts as she stirs one of the pans. "Please yourself which one."

I want to tell her that it doesn't really matter what I decide, because I won't be staying that long.

"And this young lady is my stepdaughter, Mary."

Mary's standing by the table putting the knives and forks out. She's tall, blond, and so pretty she couldn't possibly be anything else but her stepdaughter. Mary shakes my hand and says, "Hello, pleased to meet you."

"Mary won't be with us much longer now," her stepmother says. "She's getting married shortly and going to live in a flat over a barbershop in town." *Mary must be the happiest woman in Llanelli, I think to myself.*

I then get introduced to her other son, who's slouched in an armchair reading a comic. "That's John over there, he's got himself a good job making blackout curtains in the factory down the road."

John pretends he doesn't hear his mother.

"John, don't be ignorant," his mother shouts, "stop reading and say hello to Raymond."

John lowers his comic just enough to show the top part of his face, doesn't say anything, gives me a couple of slow nods, raises the comic back up, and then carries on reading. His mother shakes her head.

"Seventeen years of bloody age and here he is still reading bloody comics; he spends most of his wages on comics, silly bloody bugger."

"It won't be comics you will be reading when they get you in the army," Mary says.

"I won't be going in the army," John says, his head still behind the comic.

"You'll have to go in," Mary says. "Just like everyone else has to."

"Not according to what I've been told," John says.

"And what's that?" Mary asks.

"Because the war will be well over before I even get my calling-up papers."

"I hope to God it is," his mother says. "Then I can have my husband back."

Scruffy walks into the kitchen to sit down.

"Alan," she says (that's his real name), "take Raymond upstairs and show him his bedroom, then by the time you've done that, your dinners will be ready."

There are two beds in the room, a single and a double. The wallpaper is peeling off the damp walls, and the windowsill has a puddle of water on it where the rain has come through the hole in the window. I ask Alan which is my bed.

"We have to share this big bed," he says. "The other bed in

the corner is John's." The mother of the kittens is fast asleep in the middle of John's bed.

"SHARE?" I say, not meaning to say it aloud. "You and me?"

"Yes."

I want to run downstairs, grab my things, and run from this house as fast as I can. I'll go anywhere, even back to Mrs. Jones' house.

The responsibility of a billeting officer was to make sure that there were adequate sleeping arrangements in your billet, meaning that no child would be forced to sleep with a stranger. But Mrs. Davis had been told lies, she was told I'd have my own bed to sleep in.

Alan pokes me on my arm and says, "Did you hear what I just said?" I shake my head. I hadn't heard a word he'd said, not since he told me I was sharing a bed with him. "You'll have to le-le-leave your things in your haversack; there's no room in the drawers for your things as well as ours. And if, if, if you want to go for a pee in the night, you'll have to go to the lav outside; our po's broken." He leaves the room and goes back downstairs. It was all a nightmare, that's the only way I can explain that first day in that house.

I'm sitting on the side of the bed with my face in my hands and my haversack between my feet, wishing it were all a bad dream. I jump when his mother shouts from the bottom of the stairs, "Come on down Raymond, your dinner's ready." I hang my haversack on the back of the bedroom door and go downstairs. I feel sick inside my stomach and food is the last thing on my mind.

They are all sat around the big wooden table in the middle of the kitchen. Auntie points to my dinner and says that I can sit there next to Mary.

Hanging from a naked light bulb above the center of the table is a paper fly catcher. I notice that the heat from the stove has allowed the grungy mess of dead flies to slide to the bottom of the paper. If any drop, they're sure to land on the plate of bread that's beneath it, so I'm not eating any bread.

Just then, the cat trots in and brushes itself around my ankles, meowing for food. Alan scrapes a bit of his dinner onto a plate and puts it down on the floor.

"I hope that cat of yours wasn't on my bed spreading fleas all over it again, "John says.

Alan shakes his head and says it wasn't. John doesn't believe him and asks me if I saw the cat on his bed. I think it best not to say anything, so I just shrug my shoulders.

"The house stinks with that cat and it's kittens," Mary says.

"She's right," Auntie says. "The best place for them is in a sack in the middle of the lake."

Alan pushes his plate to one side and runs up the stairs. He's crying again. "Get down here this minute and finish your dinner," his mother shouts, "or else it goes in the bin."

He comes back down sulking.

"That'll be your job tomorrow," Auntie tells John. "You can put them in a sandbag and drown the bloody lot of them."

Alan pleads with his mother, "P-p-please don't drown them Mammy. I'll k-k-keep them under th-th-the stairs, I'll make sure they don't come out ag-ag-again."

"No," she says shaking her head. "I'm sorry, they're going. You know I hate bloody cats, I told you that when you first brought their mother here. And now look what we've got, another bloody six of them, shitting all over the bloody place."

During the meal, Auntie asks me if I know why she decided

to take in an evacuee. Although I didn't know it at the time, her only apparent motive for taking me in was to acquire extra help with the cider deliveries.

"Do you know why, Raymond?" she asks. "Did Mrs. Davis mention that to you?"

I tell her Mrs. Davis didn't mention anything about where I
was going.

"She didn't? Not even about the cider deliveries?" "No, she didn't," I tell her. "What's cider?"

Alan and John look at each other and smirk. "Did you hear that?" Alan says to John. "He doesn't even know what cider is."

I go red in the face thinking I must be the only person in the world that doesn't know what cider is.

"That's cider," Auntie says, pointing to a jug in the middle of the table. "Taste it. Go on, taste it, it's nice."

I shake my head and say no, thank you.

"You won't know until you taste it," she says, half filling a glass and pushing it over to me.

I push it back and say no, thank you, again.

"Oh well," she says putting it to her mouth, "it's no good wasting it."

As she gulps it down some runs down the side of her chin and onto her dress. She wipes her mouth with the back of her hand.

"You're going to have help the others peel some apples as well; we need plenty of them."

I tell her I don't know how to peel apples.

"You're going to have to learn," she says. "You have to earn your keep here. The ten shillings and sixpence the government pays me won't be enough to feed you."

The weekly billeting rates were:

5–10 years of age   8 shilling, 6 pence

10–14 years of age   10 shilling, 6 pence

14–16 years of age   15 shilling, 6 pence

The billetor received 10 shilling, 6 pence from the government for taking a child. Another 8 shilling, 6 pence per head was paid if the billetor took more than one child. For mothers and infants, the billetor provided lodging at a cost of only 5 shilling per adult and 3 shilling per child. This meant the mother had to arrange the buying and cooking of her own food and this often caused conflict between the billetor and evacuee.

"And it's not only the money that's the problem," Auntie says, "food is rationed now, don't you forget."

After the meal, while Mary clears the table, Auntie settles herself in a chair with the newspaper, a cigarette, and another glass of cider. John and Alan are sprawled on the couch again, reading comics. I ask if I can borrow one, but they don't answer. They don't bother to even look up.

"You can't start reading comics now," Auntie says. "I've got a couple of jobs for you to do first."

"Jobs?"

"Yes, jobs. First job is to go and help Mary in the scullery wash the dirty dishes. Then when you've finished that, I want you to fetch a bucket of coal from the shed."

I look over at John and Alan; they're laughing behind their comics.

"It's no good looking at them," she says. "Those two jobs I've just given you are your jobs from now on."

I go into the kitchen and start drying the dishes. Mary closes the door over.

"She's got no control over them," she says. "They can do whatever they like. Alan won't even help her with the cider deliveries anymore, that's why you are here. I can't wait to get married and get out of this house. I hate her and her two sons."

I tell her I don't want to live here, especially having to sleep in the same bed as Alan.

When we've finished doing the dishes, Mary gets two candles and a box of matches from the cupboard and tells me she'll help to get the coal. We go out to the coal shed at the top of the garden. Mary holds a match under each candle until it's soft enough to stick on the window ledge. We have to dig deep down into the slack with our hands to find the lumps of coal. After we've found enough lumps to fill the bucket, we fill another bucket with slack. Mary tells me that Auntie likes to put just two or three lumps on the fire and then back it up with plenty of slack, that way the fire burns slower and she saves a lot of coal. She says if I don't do it that way, Auntie will get very cross with me.

"She's got a really bad temper my stepmother, especially when she's had a lot of cider to drink."

Mary grabs a bucket in each hand and carries them into the scullery.

"Don't forget," she says, "two big lumps first then some slack. Can you manage that?"

"Yes."

"OK, I'll wait out here for you."

I carry the buckets into the kitchen and place them down on the hearth by the fire. Auntie's flopped over the side of the armchair fast asleep, her empty glass lying on the floor by her feet. Her legs have become mottled all over from the heat of the fire. John and Alan are still engrossed in their comics. John lowers his comic and tells me to put plenty of slack on. I want to tell him to put it on himself, but I'm frightened in case a row starts and I wake Auntie up, so I do as I'm told.

After I wash my hands, Mary and I go down to the bottom of the garden into the air raid shelter. She says she often goes down there because it's peaceful and quiet and she can get away from the others. Inside there are four bunk beds, one above the other on each side. At the opposite end to the door, between the bunks, is a little table, on which a wireless and a reading lamp sit. It was her father's idea; he wanted to make the shelter as comfortable as possible for them during the long air raids. He'd even covered the floor with planks of wood and laid bits of carpets on top.

Mary closes the door and lights one of the oil lamps that's hanging down above the beds. We sit on one of the bunks and talk. She tells me they had an evacuee staying with them a couple of weeks ago, but he only stayed for three days before he ran away. *I don't blame him, I say to myself.* "His name was Tommy Flint. Did you know him?"

"Yes, I do, he goes to my school. He's one of my best friends."

I had three best friends in that school—Tommy Flint, Eddie Lowe, and Jack Walters. Eddie and Jack came from Liverpool, while Tommy came from Blackburn. Tommy was a nervous, shy, elfin-size little boy with pinched features that always made him look ill. And because of the way he looked and the fact that he wouldn't stand up for himself, Tommy soon became the butt of any jokes the other kids wanted to play on him.

From left: Eddie, Jack, Paul, Me and Tommy Flint

"Why did he run away?" I asked Mary.

"My stepmother locked him under the stairs, but don't you tell anyone I told you that, otherwise you'll get me into a lot of trouble."

"Under the stairs? Why?"

"He was always peeing the bed."

The mere thought of Auntie locking me under the stairs frightens the living daylights out of me. Mary sees the concern on my face.

"Do you know how long he was under the stairs for?"

"I don't know, I wasn't in at the time, but don't you worry, she won't do it again. I've told her I'll report her to the police if she ever does anything like that again."

I know Tommy pees the bed, he told me in secret. And if it wasn't for Jennifer "Busybody" Gardener going round the class telling all the other girls about it, it would still be a secret between Tommy, Eddie, and I. I always feel sorry for Tommy, the way all the girls giggle and make fun of him. The other day I saw them all holding hands and dancing around him singing,

Shine a light, shine a light, just for a minute

So-and-so's wet the bed, and I'm lying in it.

I went up to them and pulled him out of the circle and asked Jennifer how did she know Tommy pees the bed.

"Because I live next door to him, that's why," she says in her little busy, bossy way. "So, what if you do live next door to him. How do you know he wets the bed?"

"Because every morning I see his landlady hang his mattress over the washing line to dry out."

I tell her she's a nosy poke and to mind her own business. But she doesn't care, she just laughs and sticks her tongue out at me.

Mary Gets Married

I Get My Own Bed

But Still Not Sleeping Alone

Mary tells me that when the billeting officer came and questioned her stepmother about Tommy being locked up under the stairs, she flatly denied it and said Tommy was making it all up and that she would never do such a thing. Mary says her step- mother warned her, before the billeting officer arrived, that if she said anything about it, she'd stop her brother from renting his flat to her when she gets married.

Mary and I sit talking for ages. She tells me about her job as a schoolteacher and about the boy she's engaged to. When I ask her about her father, she starts crying and tells me he's in the army somewhere abroad, and that her and her stepmother hadn't heard from him for a very long time.

"I worry about him all the time," she says. "There's already three women in this street that have lost their husbands. Whenever I see the telegram boy cycling down the street, I pray it's not our house he's coming to."

She also talks about her aunt in Swansea who now lives on her own because her husband and her two sons are fighting in the war. Mary says her aunt is terrified being on her own, especially when she's under the stairs during the air raids, which is nearly every night lately. She says the Germans have been bombing Swansea so much recently, she wonders if there's any of it still standing.

* * * * *

It's about a week after I first moved in with the Simmons' (not their real name), when I come home from school to find Mary and her stepmother bawling and shouting at each other. Mary has just told Auntie that she's pregnant. Auntie goes crazy. She tells Mary in no uncertain terms that she'll have to bring the wedding forward. Concerned about the church arrangements, Mary tells Auntie she'll go round and tell the vicar right away so he can alter the dates. "You'll do no such thing, altering dates," Auntie tells her. "You can't get married in a church now that you're pregnant; you'll have to get married in a registry office."

I walk into the kitchen just as Mary flops into a chair, her hands covering her face to hide the tears. When I ask her why she's crying, Auntie tells me to mind my own business and go out to play. It upsets me to see Mary crying so I close the scullery door and listen.

"And another thing," Auntie says. "I hope you realize you can't get married in your wedding dress now." In a broken voice Mary asks why. "You know why, because a lady doesn't get married in white when she's expecting a baby, that's why! Don't you understand that? What do you think people are going to think when they find out that you were pregnant on your wedding day?"

I hear Mary's cries getting louder. "No, no, young lady. I'm not going to let that happen, so you can forget about getting married in a church. Anyway, why you picked him in the first place is beyond me. I think he's got a big chip on his bloody shoulder that lad. In fact, when you see him next, you can tell him from me that just because he wears pants, it doesn't mean he's God's gift to women."

When I hear Mary run up the stairs sobbing, I sit on the scullery step trying to figure out why Auntie won't let her get married in her nice wedding dress.

The following month, on Mary's insistence, I'm allowed to join the rest of the family in the local registry office to see her and her boyfriend become husband and wife. Her uncle has driven her and Auntie to the church in his car; the two boys and I have to walk. After the wedding breakfast, which consisted of soup to start, followed by assorted sandwiches, then tinned pears and cream for dessert, the bride and groom are driven to their new home above Auntie's brother's barbershop in town.

I didn't get to move into Mary's bedroom—John got it. But I half expected that. Still, I'm not too disappointed; I don't have to sleep with Alan anymore.

Determination

Get Me Out Of Here

Things have got even worse since Mary left. For one thing, Auntie's started to drink cider during the day now, as well as in the evenings. And not only that, it must be at least a couple of weeks since she last washed my clothes. I know if I run away again, there's a good possibility I'll be put in an approved school for unruly boys. Mrs. Davis has promised me she'll do just that.

So for the past couple of weeks I've tried very hard to come up with some sort of plan that will induce Mrs. Davis to move me to a more suitable billet. A billet, I hope, that will be far away from Mrs. Simmons' house. But no matter how much I rack my brain, I'm not able to come up with anything that will work. Then, last Friday morning when Eddie and I are on our way to school, Eddie comes up with a brilliant idea. He says all I have to do is make a nuisance of myself by complaining about my billet all the time. At first I don't understand what he means.

"I already complain about it every Friday morning," I tell him, "when Mrs. Davis comes in and asks if anyone has a complaint about their billet."

"I know that," he says, "but what I mean is for you to complain about it every single morning, not just once a week."

"Every morning?"

"Yes, as soon as Miss Grainger finishes calling the register, you put your hand up and complain."

"But Mrs. Davis only comes on Fridays, she doesn't come every morning."

"I know that," he says, "but Miss Grainger is bound to get fed up with you complaining every single morning, isn't she?"

"Yes."

"So, to stop you complaining, all Miss Grainger has to do is make Mrs. Davis find you a new billet."

"When do you think I should start?"

"Today, start today, when Mrs. Davis comes in and asks if there are any complaints. Then again on Monday morning as soon as Miss Grainger finishes calling the register, and then every morning after that for the whole week. Tell her you don't like where you're living. Tell her how really bad it is."

And that's what I did, on that Friday morning and all last week. As soon as she'd put the register away, I jumped up from my desk and put my hand up and complained about my billet. By Wednesday, I could tell it was working because she was getting angrier each day.

But when Thursday came along, I started to get a bit scared. I told Eddie when I called for him on the way to school that I'd been worrying about ever since I'd got up out of bed that morning. I asked him if he was me, would he still carry on doing it. Eddie said he would. He said that if I didn't do it, that would mean that I'd given in, and Miss Grainger would have won. And he said you know what that means, you don't get to go to a new billet. I didn't know whether to believe Eddie or not. I wondered if he was just saying that because it gave him a good laugh every morning, just like it did with all the other kids in the class. Anyway, I did do it, but not right after she finished calling the register like I did the other mornings, I lost my nerve for a while. But I got it back again about half an hour later and did it then. Gosh, was she mad that morning!

When I woke up on the Friday morning, I was so worried about the whole thing I couldn't even eat my breakfast. But Eddie did talk me round into doing it one more time. He said she's bound to break today, which means you could be out of that billet by Monday.

After our usual Friday morning gas mask drill in the school-yard, we file into the classroom and make our way to our desks. Eddie's desk is in the back row, mine is in the next row down in front of Eddie's. We all sit with our arms folded waiting for Miss Grainger to come in. When she enters the room she looks straight at me, all slit-eyed and huffy. I know exactly what's going through her mind. When she finishes calling the register and she's putting it back in her desk, she hears a giggle coming from one of the girls in the front. She slams the lid down.

"What's the joke?" she shouts. "Who's the giggler?" No one answers.

"Whoever it was, you've got until playtime to own up. If you don't, the whole class stays in an extra hour today."

When no one comes forward, she goes over to the cupboard to get a new stick of chalk. Eddie nudges me. "Aren't you going to do it?"

I don't answer him. I don't have to; he can tell by my face what the answer is. Miss Grainger stands by the side of the black-board holding the chalk in her hand.

"I don't want to hear any complaints from anyone about their billets this morning," she says. "Does everyone hear me?"

We all nod our heads and say yes, miss. Then as she begins to write, and without bothering to turn around, she says, "Not a peep out of anyone, especially you Raymond Evans."

It's so quiet in the classroom all you can hear is the scratching noise the chalk makes on the blackboard. Then one of the boys a couple of desks in front turns around and looks at me. He cups his mouth with his hands and whispers, "Yella Belly, Yella Belly. Raymond Evans is a Yella Belly." I feel like going down and jamming his head with the desk lid.

"I'll get him at playtime," I tell Eddie. "I'll show him who's the scaredy pants."

"Do it," Eddie whispers, "otherwise they'll all make fun of you after."

I jump to my feet, stretch my arm up in the air, and shout, "EXCUSE ME, MISS."

Miss Grainger twists round, and so does everyone else. She stamps her foot on the floor like she always does when she's in a temper and shouts, "SIT DOWN."

I bend my knees to sit down, then I straighten up again. *I've got to go through with it, everyone's staring at me.* She puts her hands on her hips and rolls her eyes up to the ceiling.

"Mother of God," she says, "give me strength."

"I just want to tell you about my billet, miss, that's all."

The laughter and giggles are abruptly silenced when Miss

Grainger screams out again at the top of her voice.

"FOR GOD'S SAKE, WILL YOU SIT DOWN AND BE QUIET. I'M FED UP WITH YOU STANDING UP EVERY MORNING COMPLAINING ABOUT YOUR DAMN BILLET."

"But, miss, this billet is much worse than the last one." She throws the chalk at me. I duck and it hits the wall.

"You told me that yesterday morning, and the morning before that, AND the morning before that. NOW SIT DOWN."

"It's my landlady. You see, miss, she's always drunk." "ALWAYS DRUNK?"

"Yes, miss, she drinks cider all the time." "CIDER?"

"Yes, miss, she makes cider and sells it round the district."

Miss Grainger shakes her head. I'm sure she thinks I'm exaggerating.

"And another thing."

"And another thing WHAT?"

"And another thing, miss, the house is very, very dirty, and my bed's full of fleas all the time. Just ask Eddie, he'll tell you how dirty it is, miss, he's been in there. He thinks it's the dirtiest house he's ever been in."

All the kids are giggling and laughing as she stomps up to my desk. Her face is bright red with anger. "I've had enough of your bad behavior Raymond Evans. How many more times do I have to tell you that Mrs. Davis is trying her very best to move you as soon as she can. Now SIT DOWN AND BE QUIET."

When Mrs. Davis arrives at the school later that day, she calls me into Miss Grainger's office. *Maybe she's finally managed to find me a new billet.* I cross my fingers behind my back for good luck, but it doesn't work. "It's not going to do you any good complaining all the time about your billet," she says. "I'll find you a new place as soon as I can. You have to be patient, I've got others to look after as well as you." Disappointed and dejected, I walk out with my chin on my chest. I wonder if I'm ever going to get out of that awful house.

Christmas Parties

& Cider Loving Cockroaches

December arrives. It's my second Christmas in Llanelli. I'm thinking if it's anything like the last one, I'll not be looking forward to it. But it doesn't turn out that way, far from it. First of all there's a brand new pair of boots waiting for me at Mam's. I'm really glad about that, as my others have completely worn out. In fact, one boot is so bad, I've got to put cardboard inside to cover the hole. Then she tells me about the big party that the Royal Air Force is arranging for all the evacuees. "When is it?" I ask impatiently. "Christmas Day, of course, the twenty-fifth." She sees me trying to work out how many more days to the twenty-fifth. "It's not long," she says. "It's just around the corner."

The party is to be held at Pembrey Royal Air Force base, the camp where Dad is stationed. I'm so excited about the party. On my way home I count on my fingers how many days are left before Christmas. When I get to twenty, I start all over again. But this time, to make sure I'm counting right, I decide to count out loud. I don't care about people giving me strange looks, this is very important. I have to know before I go any further exactly how long I have to wait for the party so I can cross the days off. Twenty-one, twenty-two, twenty-three … TWENTY THREE DAYS … twenty- three whole days, that's ages and ages away. No, no, that can't be right, I must have made a mistake. One, two, three, four …

* * * * *

The trestle tables form a big square in one of the airplane hangars—there must be at least a hundred of them. At the far end stands the tallest Christmas tree I've ever seen. It must be the tallest in the world. And piled around it are hundreds and hundreds of presents. On the tables there's a party hat and a Christmas cracker at the side of every plate. When they start dishing the food out, I get told off for not waiting to pull my Christmas cracker until after the meal. I knew you weren't supposed to, Mam told us that, but I couldn't wait.

After we finish eating, there's enough turkey and Christmas pudding left over for seconds, if anybody wants it. I go back for seconds. Father Christmas gives out the presents. When that's done, we sing carols and play games. It's the best Christmas party anyone could wish for, especially being back with my sisters and brothers. I'm enjoying myself so much that I don't want it to end. But end it does, far too quickly. Before I realize what's happening, I'm back at my billet and lying in bed.

Instead of going to sleep, I pretend I'm back at the party. And as I go over every minute from start to finish, it already seems like it didn't really happen, like it was all a dream.

*****

Auntie doesn't let up on her cider drinking; it seems every time I see her she's got a bottle in her hand. And lately, because of all her drinking, she spends more time sleeping on the couch in the kitchen than she does in her bed. In fact, it's the cider that got her in trouble with the ARP Warden the other night. And that was the second time in the last two weeks. He bangs on the front door and shouts through the letterbox, "PUT THAT BLOODY LIGHT OUT. DON'T YOU KNOW THERE'S A WAR ON." We all jump out of bed, John, Alan, and me, and rush downstairs to see what's happening. When we get into the kitchen we see Auntie flat out on the couch. John shakes her as hard as he can, but it's no use, she doesn't wake up, she's dead to the world.

"It's no wonder I can't wake her," he says. "She's drank three full bottles since teatime." She's still nursing one of the empty bottles in her arms, just like she's nursing a baby to sleep. The other two bottles are lying on the floor beside the couch.

"WILL YOU SWITCH YOUR LIGHTS OUT IN THERE?" the Warden shouts through the letterbox. "YOU'RE LIGHTING ALL THE BLOODY STREET UP."

As John dashes over to the wall and switches the light off, I run up the lobby to open the front door. I can slide the bottom bolt over, but not the top one; it's too high. The Warden keeps banging on the door as John struggles with the bolt. When he finally manages to open it, the Warden steps inside the lobby and shouts in John's face, "Where is she? Bloody drunk again I suppose?"

"Yes I think so," John says. "She's on the … " John doesn't get a chance to finish, as the Warden stomps up the hallway into the kitchen, goes straight to the window, and drags the curtain closed. Then he sees Auntie—she's still flat out to the world. He stands over her, shaking his head. "I knew it," he says. "I bloody knew it would be this house the light was coming from. Even when I was at the top of the street I knew it would be this house. Well, she's not going to get away with it this time, the drunken sod, putting people's lives at risk all the time. She's had plenty of chances; now she's going to pay for it." He stomps back up the lobby and slams the door behind him.

John tries again to wake his mother up, but she just groans and turns over. He looks at the clock on the wall. Its two in the morning and that means he's only got four hours sleep left as he has to be up at six for the early shift. "Sod her," he says. "The drunken bastard. I'm fed up with her, always drunk all the time. We'll never wake her up now, no matter how much we try. I'm going back to bed, it's freezing down here. "

I run up the stairs and jump back into bed. I'm so cold with standing around, it takes ages before I finally stop shivering. Alan falls asleep almost right away, like he always does. I lay awake for ages listening to his every snore; it gets me so mad, I feel like tipping him out of his bed. I bury my head under the covers, but I can still hear his snores. When I can't stand it any longer, I get up and shake him. He looks up and grunts, "What?" "Stop snoring, I can't get to sleep." He mumbles and turns over; silence at last. But not for long. Just as I'm settling down, the clock in the parlor starts chiming, "Dong! Dong! Dong!" It's three o'clock in the morning, and I'm as wide awake as ever. I get my torch and go downstairs for a drink of water; something to do.

On my way to the scullery, I creep over to Auntie to make sure she's still asleep; both her arms are still wrapped around the empty cider bottle. When I turn the tap on in the scullery to get my drink of water, I can feel something crawling over my feet. I point the torch down to see what it is. Cockroaches!! There's a battalion of them, skittering in all directions from the torch light. I screech out, drop the glass in the sink, and make for the door. The noise wakes Auntie and she sits up and looks around. I switch the torch off and duck down behind the armchair. Some of the cockroaches must have come into the kitchen, because I can feel one on my leg. I can't help it and I screech out again. "Is there anybody there?" she asks in a slurred voice. I don't answer. She drags her legs off the couch, and still holding the cider bottle she staggers to her feet, doing a few wobbles.

"Hello, is anybody there?" she says again. I start to panic in case she puts the light on and sees me, but luckily she's still drunk and flops back down again. When I think it's safe, I run upstairs and jump back into bed. I lay awake again for ages, but this time it's not Alan's snoring that's keeping me awake, it's the sight of all those cockroaches in the kitchen. I keep switching the torch on and shining it on the bottom of the door in case they've come up the stairs.

* * * * *

January turns into February, and February turns into March, and I still haven't moved. It's a Saturday morning, the morning when I have to help Auntie with the cider deliveries. The reason Alan refused to help this morning is because it's freezing cold and raining very heavy, so Auntie lets him stay in his nice warm bed.

When I get downstairs, Auntie has wheeled the cart into the scullery and is loading it with bottles of cider. As soon as I finish eating my breakfast, we get on our way to the first customer, Auntie in front, me behind pushing the cart. We are halfway to the first house when I ask Auntie if I can go back for my gloves, my fingers are stiff with the cold. Although I only have to run to the top of the street, she refuses to let me go. "It's your own fault for forgetting them," she says.

At our first stop, a little further down the street, the lady orders her usual two small bottles. Auntie shouts from the lady's step, "Bring two small bottles." I pick two out of the cart, and instead of carrying them in my hands, I jam one in each pocket of my jacket and hold on to them as I run up the path. One slips out of my hand as I'm passing them to the lady and it smashes onto her path. Auntie gets very upset; she hates it when I break one of her bottles of cider. I say that I'm sorry and bend down to pick up the broken glass.

"You stupid boy, I've told you before not to carry them in your pocket. Leave the glass where it is, I'll pick it up myself. Go and get another bottle, and don't carry it in your pocket this time." It's not until I get back to the cart that I realize I've cut my finger. It's started to sting with the rain, and it's bleeding very heavily. When I get back with the other bottle, the customer notices my finger bleeding. She takes me into her house, sits me by the fire, and puts a bandage on it. When I get up to leave, she tells me to sit down and stay where I am. I wonder what she's going to do. "I'll be back in a second," she says. "Just stay there." When she comes back she says, "It's alright, I've told Mrs. Simmons that your clothes are too wet to carry on with the deliv- eries, and that she can pick you up later."

"No, I have to help her," I say. "She'll get mad with me if I don't."

"I don't think she will," she says, "but just in case she does, you come and tell me right away." I didn't know it at the time, but this particular lady worked for the local council and part of her job was the welfare of the evacuees.

She gives me a dressing gown and leaves me alone in the kitchen to take my wet clothes off. I'm sitting by the fire when she comes back in carrying a cup of cocoa and a plate of biscuits. "Here, drink this," she says. "It'll warm you up." After she's finished draping my clothes over the fireguard, she pulls a chair up and sits alongside me.

"Do you like where you're living, Raymond?" she asks.

"No," I tell her. "I don't. I hate it."

"Have you asked the billeting officer to move you?"

"Plenty of times, but she can't find anywhere."

"It's very hard to find homes at the moment," she says. "There are lots of evacuees coming into Llanelli again."

"Do you take evacuees in?"

"Yes."

"Will you take me in?"

"I'm sorry, Raymond," she says. "I already have two evacuees, two little girls."

Another one of Auntie's customers I asked to take me in was a lady who I assumed lived on her own. She was a nice old lady who gave me a penny every time we delivered to her house. She'd slide it into my pocket when Auntie was looking the other way, then pat me on my head and give me a quick wink.

So that none of Auntie's customers will see me, I go round the back of her house and knock on her scullery door. As I stand waiting, I cross my fingers behind my back and whisper, *Please, please God, make her take me in.*

"Hello Raymond," she says, in her deep Welsh accent. "What are you doing here?"

"I've come to ask if you'll take me in. I don't want to stay with Mrs. Simmons anymore."

"Take you in?" she asks. "You mean to live here with me?"

"Yes, it won't be for long, it might even be just for a few months."

"A few months?"

"Yes, that's all. The war will be finished soon you see."

"The war? Finished soon? I don't think so."

"It will. Everyone's saying it."
"You better come in," she says. "It's cold out there."

I get a shock when I get into the kitchen—one of Auntie's friends is sitting at the table drinking tea.

She's bound to tell her I've been here.

"Hello Raymond, she says. "Did I hear you say something about the war finishing soon?

"Er, yes."

"Where did you hear that?"

The fact being that I'd just made it up on the spur of the moment, I decide to ignore her.

"I'll run messages and do anything you want me to," I say to the old lady.

"You live with Mrs. Simmons, don't you?" the other lady asks. "Yes."

"Why do you want to leave there then?"

I don't want to tell her why, so I ignore her again.

"I'm sorry Raymond," the old lady says. "All my time is taken up looking after my husband, he's very ill you see."

I look round for her husband.

"He's not down here," she says. "He's upstairs and can't get out of bed you see Raymond."

I realize at this point that it's pointless me staying any longer. "OK," I say. "Thank you. I have to go now."

When I get to the door, I whisper in the old lady's ear and ask her to ask her friend not to tell Mrs. Simmons about me coming to her house. She squeezes a penny in my hand and whispers, "OK, I'll tell her not to mention it."

Stark Naked In The

"Scabby Hole"

One of my worst memories I have of those days was to wake up one morning and find that I'd caught a horrible disease called scabies. It happened during my stay with the Simmons' - twice as a matter of fact.

The spread of scabies in Wales during those early years of the war, which at one time reached epidemic proportions, was generally attributed to the incoming stream of evacuees. Medical reports in Liverpool showed that scabies was on the increase, mostly in the poorer areas, long before the war had started. And because of the hot atmosphere and the tightly packed carriages, the twelve-hour journey that our train took to get to Llanelli gave the highly contagious scabies mite plenty of time to thrive.

I'd been evacuated about 18 months, and up until then, unlike most of the evacuees I knew, I had managed to stay clear of it.

* * * * *

I sit up in bed and examine my body—it's everywhere. It's between my fingers, between my toes, even under my arms.

Two days later the billeting officer takes me to a special hostel, or "scabby hole" as it's often termed by some of the Welsh kids.

When we arrive, the billeting officer passes me over to a nurse who immediately takes me to the treatment room. On the table I notice a very large jar of bright, yellowy ointment (sulpher ointment), a shaving brush, and a pair of barber's hair clippers. She sits me in a chair and covers my shoulders with a white cloth.

"Are you going to shave my head?" I ask.

"Yes, I'm afraid so" she says, picking the clippers up. "But don't worry, it'll soon grow back."

When she's finished, she tells me to strip off.

"Take my clothes off?"

"Yes, and stand on this sheet of brown paper."

"All my clothes?"

"Yes, all of them."

I stop when I get to my underpants, thinking that maybe she'll let me leave them on.

"And your underpants."

"My underpants as well?"

"Yes, your underpants as well, everything."

I can feel my face getting redder and redder as I slide the last bit of clothing from my naked body. And this, I have to say, has to be the most humiliating, shameful, and embarrassing moment

I've had to face up until this point in my life. And the worst of it all is, according to what the other kids have told me who've already been in here, I have to have the ointment treatment not just this once, but twice a day until the rash has disappeared.

"I'm sorry," she says, as she scoops a dollop of ointment onto the shaving brush. "This is going to burn for a few minutes, OK?"

I clench my fists, squeeze my eyes closed, and whimper, "OK."

She starts with my head, and then goes onto my chest and back, and down to my legs. Before she gets to my feet, the burning sensation on my head has become so intense that I feel like someone has taken it off my shoulders, boiled it, and put back on again. And when the burning reaches my chest and back, I want to tell her to stop, I can't take it much longer. She can call me a coward if she wants, I don't care, just as long as she stops. I've always been a coward as regards medicines and pain. In fact, Mam would be the first one to tell anyone that. I remember once when she was applying iodine to my cut knee, I was shouting "Ow!" even before she got the cork out of the bottle. "For God's sake," she said. "You're crying and I haven't even touched you yet."

"There, we've finished with the ointment," the nurse says, "you can open your eyes now, and stop biting your lip, you'll make it bleed."

After sticking strips of plaster over my fingernails to stop me from scratching, she takes a very, very large nightshirt out of a cupboard and tells me to get dressed. The nightshirt is so large that there's enough room for at least another three people to fit inside. "It's the wrong size," I tell her. "Can I have a smaller one?" "They're all the same size," she says. "That's all we have. They're to prevent the ointment sticking to your skin." I feel like I'm walking inside of a tent as I follow her into the ward.

I lay in bed staring up at the ceiling. Under my arms and in my groin, the ointment is still burning.

"What's your name?" a voice comes from the next bed.

I turn my head and say Ray. I'm sorry I answered him because he gets up and sits on the side of his bed to talk.

"Has it stopped burning yet

Ray?" "Yes," I reply, "just about."

"You get it twice a day you know."

"I know," I answer. "Someone told me before I came

in." "I've had it twice a day for six days now."

"Have you?" I answer, trying not to sound disinterested.

"Yeah, I only have to have it two more days the nurse says, then I can go out."

"Mmmm, lucky for you then isn't it?"

He gets up and pulls his chair over to my bed. "Just two more days, that's all," he says. "Then I'll be out of here."

I wish it was today. I've only been in here ten minutes and you're already getting on my nerves. Telling me you've only got two more days when I've got two weeks in this scabby hole.

I slide away from him and close my eyes pretending I'm going to sleep. It does the trick, and he gets up, checks to see if the nurse is around, then walks across the ward to speak to some-one else. It's the first time I get a proper look at him. He looks so funny in his big nightshirt, with his orange-coloured head, I have to cover my mouth so he can't hear me laughing. Then I realize I must look the same. So I get up and go to the bathroom and look in the mirror. I can't believe it's me; I look like someone that has escaped from a mental asylum.

Later that week Dad, who happens to be on leave, comes in to see me. I get a shock when I see him come into the ward because I'd been told by the other kids that we weren't allowed visitors. But the reason Dad was allowed to see me was that he was about to be posted overseas to the Middle East in the next few days. "It's just for a few minutes," the nurse told him. "Just as long as you stay clear of the bed."

All the other kids stare at Dad because he's in his Royal Air Force uniform, which makes me feel very proud of him. I point to my head and say (as if he hasn't already noticed), "They've cut it all off." He smiles and says, "Don't worry about it, it'll grow back."

Just before he leaves, he takes a big bar of Cadbury's chocolate from his pocket and throws it on my bed. "Thanks, Dad," I say. "I love Cadbury's chocolate, haven't had it for ages." "Share it with the others," he says. "Don't eat it all yourself." I ask him if he'll be coming in again to see me. "No," he says. "I won't be able to. I'll be going away for a while." A big lump comes in my throat. "How long are you going for?" I ask him, trying my best to hold the tears back. "Only for a few months," he says. "Not long." Dad was just saying that, as he really didn't know how long it would be. In fact, it would be another three and a half years before I would see him again, in 1945, when the war finally came to an end.

A few months later, things get even worse. I get up one morning to find my breakfast reduced to a small dish of cornflakes and hot water instead of milk. "It's due to the rationing," she tells me. "I can't even get the odd tin of condensed milk like I used to."

I have hunger pains all that day in school. So, when the four o'clock bell rings, I dash out of the classroom and run all the way home for my dinner. But, when I get there, all I get is two slices of bread and dripping and a cup of tea with no sugar or condensed milk. I don't know what everyone else has had, but because of the smell of meat and potatoes that's still lingering in the kitchen, I have a feeling it's not been bread and dripping they've been eating. I tell Auntie I'm still hungry and ask if there's anything else to eat. She gives me a plate of hot porridge. I'd enjoy it a lot more if there was sugar or condensed milk on it, but I'm so hungry it doesn't bother me.

As I'm eating, she goes on about the rationing again, explaining how everyone is allowed only a certain amount of food. She tells me that the reason I've been given bread and dripping sandwiches for my dinner is because I've already this week used up most of my weekly rations. I tell her I don't know what she means. She gets up from the table, goes over to the pantry, and starts to take things from the shelves. When she comes back to the table, she places before me the remainder of my weekly rations, which consist of a tiny square of butter, a tiny square of cheese, a tiny portion of tea, and a tiny portion of jam. There were a couple of other things, but I can't remember what they were.

"We all have to be very careful how we use our rations," she says, picking them up to take them back to the pantry. "Otherwise, if we use them up too early we won't have anything to eat until the following week. That's why you only had bread and dripping for dinner today."

Instead of mixing all the rations together to make them go further, like most other people did in those days, this lady, for some reason, decided to start separating mine from theirs. Luckily for me, it only lasted a couple of days. I don't know what changed her mind, but a couple of days later I was allowed to sit down with the rest of the family at dinnertime and eat a proper meal again. But it was only dinnertime when I was given a proper meal. For breakfast she continued to put only hot water on my cornflakes, never fresh or condensed milk. She even stopped giving me sandwiches for lunch.

Mrs. Jones always mixed the rations together. For instance, she'd put everyone's tiny portion of butter and margarine in a bowl, add a drop of milk, and whip it all up with a fork because it lasted twice as long that way.

The following are the permitted weekly rations of certain basic foodstuffs:

4 oz. of bacon	2 oz. tea
2 oz. of butter	4 oz. margarine
6 oz. of sugar	1 egg

*****

Hardly a few weeks had gone by before I caught scabies again, landing me back in the "scabby hole" for the second time. And although I wasn't looking forward to having to go through the head shaving and ointment treatment again, the thought of being given three proper meals each day actually made it worthwhile.

But already, just three weeks after leaving hospital, I've lost the little bit of weight I gained while I was in there; I'm back to looking pale and skinny again. And what's worse, I can't cope with the hunger bouts the same as I was able to before I went in.

The first week out of hospital was the worst. I was so hungry one day that I stole a pork pie from a butcher's counter in the market. I knew he hadn't seen me do it because I made sure his back was turned. The problem was, I wasn't sure if anyone else had seen me running away with it. For a whole week I worried about it day and night, wondering if anybody had actually recognized me. Every morning, the first thing that entered my head as I threw the bed clothes back was a picture of a policeman standing at the school gates waiting for me. But I've finally stopped worrying about it this last week or so. I'm sure if anyone had seen me doing it, surely I would have known about it long before now.

Escape To The

Saturday Matinee

It's about eleven o'clock on a freezing cold Saturday morning. Auntie and I have just walked in from the cider round. John lit the fire before he left for work this morning, so the house is lovely and warm. Before I do anything else, I want to sit in the armchair in front of it so I can thaw out my hands and feet. But Auntie says I can warm myself after I've filled the bucket with coal, otherwise the fire will get too low. Alan is still in bed. *Why doesn't she make him get the coal instead of me.*

After I've backed the fire up, I sit looking at the flames, thinking about the tips the customers have given me today—three whole pennies, the most I've ever had in one single day. That means I can go to the pictures this afternoon and still have a penny left to spend on something else. I don't want Auntie to find out about the tips, because last time she took the money out of my pocket and made me split it with Alan, and he doesn't even come on the cider round. So since that happened, I've always hid the tips down my socks.

When she finishes her cup of tea and cigarette, she goes upstairs to wake Alan up. This gives me the opportunity to grab my coat and gas mask from under the stairs and sneak out before she comes down. I only get as far as the garden gate when I hear her shout.

"Hey, where are you going?"

I turn round wondering where the voice is coming from. "Up here," she shouts. "I'm up here in the bedroom."

I look up and see her leaning out of the bedroom window. "Where are you sneaking off to?"

"I'm going to my mother's, Auntie. I won't be long." "Have you filled the coal bucket?"

"Yes."

"Are you sure? Don't you go out without filling the coal bucket."

"I have Auntie, and I've backed the fire up with slack." I close the gate and start walking.

"Just a minute, young fellow," she shouts. "Come back here."

I walk back to the gate. She has a very suspicious look on her face.

"Yes, Auntie?"

"Why are you going to your mother's on a Saturday?" "Just for a change, Auntie, that's all."

"I think you're telling fibs."

"I'm not, honest."

"Yes you are you, lying little sod. I can tell by your face you're telling fibs, and you know what happens to little boys who tell fibs."

"I'm not telling fibs, Auntie. I am going to my mother's."

"You've never been to your mother's on a Saturday since you came here."

"I know, but I haven't been to see her for a long time, so I
thought I better go today."

"I think you're going round to that market again, that's what
I think."

"No, I'm not. I'm not going round the market."

"To the pictures then, that's where you're going, isn't it? To the pictures."

"No, Auntie, I've got no money to go to the market or the pictures."

"I think you have got money, and I've a good idea where from. You stay there until I come down, and don't you dare move."

She slams the window down. I don't wait around. I sprint up the street and out of sight before she reaches the garden gate. And just in case she sends Alan after me, I climb over old Tom Smith's wall, dash across his vegetable plot, and crouch behind his tool shed. When the coast is clear, I get up and make my way to Eddie's house to see if he wants to go for a walk around the market with me.

"No" he says. "I'm not going to the market. I've only got enough money for the pictures."

"I've got thruppence," I tell him. "Tuppence for the pictures, and a penny for a bag of broken biscuits. I'll share them with you if you come with me."

"Naa," he says, shaking his head. "You eat them. I'm not hungry, my landlady gives me plenty to eat."

"You're lucky," I tell him. "I wish I had a billet like yours."

"Why don't you run away," he says. "You're always saying you want to."

"I'm scared of Mrs. Davis."

"I wouldn't have stayed half the time you have," he says. "Especially with a dirty cow like her. I'll see you outside the cinema later."

The queue outside the baker's where I buy my broken biscuits is so long it not only stretches past three other shops, but right around the corner as well; it could take hours before I get served, and that can only mean one thing—no pictures. I glance over to the grocer's, as sometimes he has broken biscuits, but it's the same there. I'm starving. I've got to get something to eat, but what can I get for a penny? I walk further down the street and stop when the butcher's shop comes into view (the same butcher I stole the pie from).

I step back and hide in a shop doorway while he finishes pasting his poster on the window outside.

Fresh Today!

Pork pies 3d each (meat coupons required)

Only two pies to each family.

My idea of a perfect afternoon in those days, when I had the money, was being able to go to the Dock Cinema on Station Road and watch the Saturday matinee. But I'm so hungry on this particular day that I'd willingly give up going to the pictures and spend my three pennies on a pie instead. I take another look at the queue and do a quick count to see whether it's worth joining. With sixty or seventy people still to go, he might not have enough pies left for everyone. That's always happening; it happened to me many a time when I was shopping for Mrs. Jones. Standing for three hours in the freezing cold and then getting right up to the counter to be told, "I'm sorry, we're sold out." I turn and walk away. Maybe it's just as well, I say to myself, someone might have recognized me anyway.

I'm already outside the cinema, reading the posters on the wall, when Eddie rolls up. I tell him a Popeye cartoon is on first, followed by a Gene Autry film. I'm really happy about that, as Gene Autry is definitely my favorite out of all the cowboys. So for the next two hours or so, just like most Saturdays, I can go into my little fantasy world and forget about Mrs. Simmons and all my problems.

When the film is finished, me and Eddie go outside and pretend we're cowboys. We always do that whenever there's a cowboy film on. I'm Gene, and he's Hop-a-long Cassidy. He keeps asking me if we can swap, so he can be Gene for a change. "Next Saturday," I tell him. "You can be Gene next Saturday."

"Next Saturday? It's always next Saturday," Eddie says. "And when next Saturday comes, you still won't swap." Really, I suppose it's only fair to swap names being that Eddie's my best friend, but the name Hop-a-long Cassidy is a name that doesn't really appeal to me like Gene Autry's name does. I mean ... a cowboy named Hop-a-long?

When we get outside the cinema, we go over to an imaginary hitching rail, untie the imaginary reins, pull ourselves on to our imaginary saddles, and gallop all the way home on our imaginary horses. After Eddie and I have parted company and I get to the house, I slide off the imaginary saddle and tie the imaginary horse to the garden gate. I'm swaggering up the path when I see Auntie standing in the scullery doorway with her arms tightly folded across her chest. She's got a face like thunder. When I get to the door she snarls at me through her teeth.

"Where've you been?"

"To my mother's."

"No you haven't. You haven't been to your mother's, you liar."

"I have Auntie, honest."

"No you haven't. Don't tell lies. You've been to the pictures because someone saw you in the queue and told me."

I go red in the face and look down.

"I thought so. I knew you were telling lies. Now where did you get the money from to go to the pictures?"

"Someone on the cider round gave it me."

"You're telling lies again, aren't you? You didn't get the money from the cider round."

"I did Auntie, that's the truth.

She bends from the waist, grabs my arms, and shakes me. "You're a bloody little liar Raymond Evans, that's what you are. You stole that money from my purse."

"From your purse? No, I didn't Auntie, honest I didn't. I really got it from a customer on the cider round."

"Have you got any more money in your pockets?"

"No, I spent what I had on the pictures."

"All of it?"

"I only had thruppence ... tuppence for the pictures and a penny I spent on some licorice sticks."

"I still think you're lying. Take your coat off while I search you."

She searches my coat pockets, and when she doesn't find anything she drags it off me and throws it across the room. Then she kneels down to search the pockets of my pants. Nothing in them, either. She turns me around to face her. I'm looking straight into her eyes and they're full of pure hatred. "You're telling me lies, you lying little sod. I know you are. Now WHERE'S THE BLOODY MONEY?"

"I don't know. Please believe me, I didn't steal any money."

"Right, that's it," she screams, pointing to the cupboard under the stairs. "I've had enough. You're going in there."

My insides turn to jelly as she grabs me and pulls me over to the cupboard. "Please Auntie, not in there. Please, please don't lock me in there."

She presses her hand on the back of my head and pushes me in. "Get in there, you little bastard, and you'll not be let out until you own up?"

She slams the door shut and pushes an armchair against it.

It's pitch black everywhere. I can't see a thing, not even a crack of light around the door. I bang my fists as hard as I can against the door, screaming for someone to come and get me out.

"You can bang as much as you like, there's no one else here, only me, and I'm going out now." I stop and listen to see if she really is going out. I hear her footsteps fade away along the hall-way to the front door.

Yes, she really is going out and leaving me here. I'll tell her it was me that stole the money, it'll be worth it just to get out of here.

"AUNTIE, CAN YOU HEAR ME? IT WAS ME WHO TOOK THE MONEY. PLEASE LET ME OUT."

It's too late. The front door slams shut.

I lie on my back to try and push the door open with my feet, but it's no use, it won't even budge. Then I get back on all fours and try feeling round for something that will pry the door open, but there's nothing but junk, old shoes, and discarded clothing. Getting more frustrated, I lie on my back and I try again with my feet, but it still won't open, the armchair is far too heavy to move.

I sit and lean against the wall with my knees under my chin. Tears start to roll down my face again; this time it's tears of frustration. Frustration at being treated like some animal she's locked up in a cage. Why doesn't Mrs. Davis find me somewhere else to live, she knows how bad it is here, I've told her about it often enough. She's like all the others—they only pretend to care.

After sitting crunched up for what seems like hours, the anger begins to boil up inside me again. I cup my hands around my mouth and shout as loud as I can for someone to get me out. Maybe some-one next door or in the street might hear me. But it's no use, all I can hear is the faint ticking of the clock on the mantelpiece.

The foul smell that the kittens have left behind has become so overwhelming that it's beginning to make me feel sick. Then suddenly I hear a noise. I hold my breath.

Yes it's someone coming in, I can hear them opening the front door. I hear Mary's voice. She must have come to let me out.

"Mary, Mary, I'm in here." She runs down the hallway and drags the armchair away from the door. I crawl out on my hands and knees and stand up, rubbing my eyes. Mary takes me by my arm, and leads me into the kitchen. Auntie and Alan are sitting on the couch. "I'm sorry Raymond," Auntie says. "It was Alan that stole the money. I'm really very sorry."

"Alan came round to my house," Mary says. "He told me he

was too frightened to tell his mother."

"I hate you," I say to Auntie. "I'm going to tell everyone what you did to me, and what you did to Tommy." Mary grabs me by my arm and takes me upstairs. We sit on the side of the bed. She puts her arm around me.

"Now listen Raymond, I know you're thinking of running away, and I can't blame you for wanting to, but I don't want you to do that. It will just get you into more trouble. Wait until Monday, until I go to the school and see Mrs. Davis so she can find you a new place first."

"Will I get moved on Monday?"

"If not Monday, it'll be later in the week."

"Are you going to tell Mrs. Davis about Auntie locking me under the stairs? Because she won't believe me, I know she won't."

"Yes."

"You really mean it?"

"I do, as long as you promise not to run away. It's only for a few days, that's all."

"OK, I won't run away."

Cornflakes And Condensed Milk

I lay awake for ages that night hoping nothing will go wrong at the meeting on Monday with Mary and Mrs. Davis. I put my head under the covers in case Alan hears me, and ask God to help find me a new billet. I asked him to find me a billet with nice people. Nice people with a nice, clean house and not dirty like this one I'm in now. And when I've finished, I decide to start all over again, just in case he was busy listening to someone else's problems. And when I wake up during the night, I ask him again in case he's forgotten. Then I ask him two more times on Sunday, just to make sure. Once when I'm in the toilet, and once when I'm on my own in the scullery washing the dishes. Please God I ask, pleeeease, please don't forget, because if you do, this time I'll run so far away no one will ever find me. Sunday night, the same again. This time I ask not just twice before I go to sleep, but at least six times. I ask him to tell Mary not to take any notice of Mrs. Davis if she tells her that I should stay in this billet.

Please listen to me God, because I know what she'll say to Mary. She'll say, "I don't believe a word of it, he'll do or say anything to get moved from that billet. I know what Mrs. Davis is like God. She'll tell Mary that it's just another one of his exaggerated stories he got from Tommy Flint.

A bad dream wakes me up during the night. I dream that Mrs. Simmons has locked me under the stairs again and I've been in there for a whole week. And when people come to find me, she tells them that I've run away and she doesn't know where I am.

Alan is snoring his head off as usual. I try to go back to sleep, but I can't. Mrs. Davis keeps coming into my mind. I can see her sitting in Miss Grainger's office later this morning. She's telling Mary that she can't move me today because she's got too many other evacuees to see to. She's telling Mary that it could be weeks or even months before she can move me.

Well I don't care what you think Mrs. Davis, I've made up my mind this time. I'm not going to stay here. I'm going to get up and run away right now.

So, on an early Monday morning late in January 1941, I slide from under the sheets, get dressed, pack my haversack with all my worldly goods, grab my gas mask from behind the bedroom door, and sneak quietly down the stairs to freedom. But before I leave, I have to put my little plan into place, the one I thought up while I was lying in bed.

I go into the kitchen, pick a chair up, and take it over to the pantry to stand on so I can reach the top shelf. The top shelf is Auntie's secret hiding place where she keeps (among other things that she doesn't want me to know about) the condensed milk and the sugar. I have to stand on tiptoes to reach because she always keeps the condensed milk and sugar hidden away in a metal biscuit tin right at the back of the shelf behind some other stuff. All that's in there when I open it is the half can of condensed milk, no sugar. I don't expect to see any sugar because most of the time she always uses her ration coupons on condensed milk instead.

She thinks I don't know about her little hiding place, but I have known ever since the first week I came here. And there's something else she doesn't know. Well, at least not until later this morning when she gets up that is. She doesn't know that while she's snoring her head off, I'm going to sit here and eat every single drop of her condensed milk. Then, when she comes down and sees the empty can on the table, she and her two sons will know what it's really like to eat cornflakes with just hot water on.

When I finish scraping the bottom of the can, I place it in the middle of the table.

I don't think she'll take me back now, not when she sees this empty can.

As promised, Mary went to the school on the Monday morning and met with Mrs. Davis. After they'd been talking for a while, Mrs. Davis came into the classroom and called me into her office. She was very angry, and so was Mary.

"Why did you run away?" Mary asks. "You made a promise that you wouldn't. I'm very annoyed with you."

I tell her I'm sorry.

"Now listen to me," Mrs. Davis says. "Just to teach you a lesson, I've a good mind to go and see Mrs. Simmons right now and ask her to take you back."

"Take me back? I'll never go back there. She locked me under the stairs."

"I know she locked you under the stairs, Mary told

me." "She did it to Tommy Flint as well."

"I know she did it to Tommy as well, Mary's just told me all about it, but you shouldn't have run away. How on earth do you expect me to find you a new billet on such short notice?"

"I don't know. I just don't want to go back to that

house." A few minutes later, Miss Grainger comes in.

"Raymond," she says. "I've just received some very exciting news from your mother."

"You mean she's letting me move in with her?"

"No, no, you're not moving back with your mother. You have a new baby brother." I stand looking at her with my mouth open, unable to take in what she's just told me.

"A new baby brother?"

"Yes, his name's David. Isn't that wonderful news? You'll be able to go and see him in a couple of days."

Dejection is written all over my face. "I don't want to see him."

"You don't want to see your new baby brother? Why not for heaven's sake?"

"Because I don't."

Disappointed at the fact that my mother has suddenly found room in her billet for another new brother, a lump grows in my throat the size of an apple.

I was little more than eight and a half years old at the time, and a lot more naive than the children of the same age today. I was made to believe that a baby came by "special request." I truly thought that once my mother had decided what sex she wanted her baby to be, it was just a matter of waiting a few months until a stork picked one up from ... err, well, wherever he picked one up from. Then all he had to do was to deliver it. I kept asking myself the same question, over and over again, "If Mam doesn't have room for me, why has she sent for another baby?"

On that same day, the "Nit Nurse" happened to pay her weekly visit to the school. She comes to check if any of the children have head lice, or "nits" as we call them. I don't know her proper name because she's always referred to as "Nitty Nora,the Nit Explorer." I knew she was coming that day, just like everyone else did, because about an hour before she arrived we saw the monitor bring the screen and a chair out of Miss Grainger's office and place them in the corner of the classroom. That's where the nurse always does her examinations.

When Nitty Nora enters the classroom and settles herself down on her chair, we all get up from our desks and line up, ready to be called in. I've been dreading the Nit Nurse coming for a long time because I've got nits now. I must have caught them off Alan, because I didn't have them before I moved into his house. In fact, I've never had nits. This is the first time.

"Next. Come on in … quickly now," the nurse shouts in her sharp, demanding voice.

It's my turn, so I go behind the screen and stand in front of her while she gets a new form from her case.

"Name?"

"Raymond Evans,

miss." "Age?"

"Eight, miss."

"Right. Kneel down on the floor and bend your head …quickly now."

With her fingers she begins to part my hair, first on the top, then on the sides, and then on the back.

"How long have you been like this

Raymond?" "Don't know, miss."

"Have you had them for a short while, or have you had them for a long time?"

"A long time, miss."

"Have you had them since you moved into the billet you're in now or before?"

"Since I moved in with Mrs. Simmons,

miss." "The billet you're in now?"

"Yes, miss."

"Right. Stand up and go in the other room. Quickly now. I'll be in shortly."

I go in the other room where there are several other kids silently waiting for her to come in and start the delousing.

After I've had my head washed with some foul smelling liquid, I'm sent back to the classroom. And as I walk past the other kids, the kids that don't have nits, I hear them whispering to each other, "Here comes Raymond Evans, nitty head. Ha, ha, ha!"

The end of lessons bell rings just as Mrs. Davis comes out of Miss Grainger's office. She's been in there most of the day. Miss Grainger tells me to stay at my desk and not to go out to play. A few minutes later, Nitty Nora comes flying into the classroom, heads straight for Miss Grainger's office, and, without knocking, barges straight in. A lot of shouting and arguing starts, mainly between the nurse and Mrs. Davis. It's so loud that I can hear everything, even though I'm quite a distance from the door.

The nurse's voice was the loudest. "Mrs. Davis," she shouts. "He has head lice, his underclothes are filthy dirty, and he's got cardboard inside his boots to cover the holes in them." (The boots that the nurse is referring to are Alan's old boots. He's wearing my new boots that my mother has recently bought me.) "And furthermore," she continues, "except for his face, I don't think the rest of his body has seen soap and water for at least two weeks."

Mrs. Davis, trying to get a word in, says, "But I've tried to find ... "

"I know it's difficult," the nurse interrupts, "but he should've never been allowed to stay there more than a few days, never mind fifteen months. You'll have to find him somewhere else, Mrs. Davis. I won't allow you to take him back to the Simmons'."

"I wasn't intending to send him back," Mrs. Davis says. "The problem is, I just don't know where to put him tonight."

"I might have someone that may help," Miss Grainger says. "It's a lady I stayed with for a short while when I first arrived in Llanelli. I'll give her a ring."

When she finished making the call, she comes out of the office with Mrs. Davis and Nitty Nora and says (much to Mrs. Davis' delight), "Mrs. Abelson agrees to take him in, but it'll only be a temporary stay."

"Well, it will at least allow you a little more time to find him a new billet," the nurse says, nodding to Mrs. Davis.

"Yes, it will," Mrs. Davis says meekly. "I'll find him some-where by then."

The notice on the big iron gate says, "Private! Trespasses will be Prosecuted." Miss Grainger ignores it and pushes one of the giant gates open just wide enough for us to get through. After she closes it, we proceed to walk along the winding gravel driveway toward the house.

We seem to be walking for ages when suddenly a very large stone building comes into view. It's big and high like a mansion, and it has lots of windows. I stop and stare at it.

I've been tricked, I say to myself. She's putting me in a home.

I pull my hand away from Miss Grainger's. "What's the matter?" she asks. "What's wrong?"

"It's a home for bad children, isn't it? You're putting me in there because you think I stole Mrs. Simmons' money. Well I'm not going in. I didn't steal the money. I'll run away."

She grabs my arm and kneels in front of me."It's not a home," she says. "It's your new billet. No one's putting you in a home. We know you didn't steal the money."

"It looks like a home. It's so big."

"Well, it's not. It belongs to Mr. and Mrs.

Abelson. "How many people live there?"

"Mr. and Mrs. Abelson and their helper, Nancy, that's all. She's a nice girl, Nancy, you'll like her. She comes all the way from Dublin."

When we get closer my eyes fix onto the stone gargoyle above the center door. I wonder why anyone would want to have an ugly face like his stuck on the front of their house.

Miss Grainger pulls on a cord that hangs from a hole at the side of the door. It rings a bell inside. A young girl opens the door, maybe sixteen or seventeen. *Must be Nancy.* She recognizes Miss Grainger. "Mrs. Abelson's in the conservatory," she says in her Irish accent. "Would yer please follow me now." We step out of the vestibule into a very large room. A room large enough, I'm sure, to fit the whole of my last billet in. "This way," Nancy says. "Through here."

As we cross the room I begin to wonder what Mrs. Abelson

is going to think when she sees that I've been treading her immaculate carpets and rugs in these shabby, holey boots. Maybe when she sees me she'll change her mind and ask Mrs. Grainger to take me back and find me somewhere else to live.

When we come out of there, we're taken through into another room just as big and grand as the previous one. This one has wood paneled walls, magnificent stained glass windows, and, hanging over the center of a very long table, a large crystal chandelier. It's a far cry from the naked light bulb that hung over the Simmons' kitchen table. The door that leads out of there takes us through into yet another room that leads to the conservatory. My heart thumps louder and louder as we get nearer and nearer to where Mrs. Abelson is waiting.

She's sat typing behind a big, wooden, roll-top desk. A pretty lady in her mid-forties, she's got short black hair and big brown eyes. She stops and peers over her glasses, smiles, and says, "Hello." I stand in front of her, looking down at the floor, red-faced and motionless. Miss Grainger tells me to look up and not be shy. I want to, but am too embarrassed to show my red face. Mrs. Abelson pushes her glasses onto her forehead, slides off her chair, takes hold of my hand, and in a low voice says,

"How about telling me your last name then Raymond?"

"Evans," I murmur at the floor.

"I'm sorry, what was that you said

Raymond?" "Evans," I repeat more firmly.

"Well, it's nice to have you here, Raymond Evans. We've been looking forward to you coming here, my husband and I. We don't have any children of our own, you see, so it will be nice to have one around the place. Do you think you'll like it here?"

My face begins to cool off. I look up at her smiling

face. "Do you? Do you think you'll like it here then?"

"Yes, miss, I do. I am going to like it here."

Nancy takes me upstairs to my bedroom while my landlady and Miss Grainger settle in the lounge over a cup of tea. "Come on, Raymond," she says as she grabs my haversack and gas mask. "Follow me." I try to keep up with her as she gallops along the landing. By the time I get to the bedroom, she's dropped my things on the bed, trotted into the bathroom, and turned the bath taps on. When she comes out, I'm standing in the middle of the bedroom, looking up at the ceiling, mesmerized at it's colourful, exquisite moldings.

"While you're having your bath, I'll put all your things away," Nancy says. "I've started running the water." I sit on a chair in the corner of the room to take my boots off, still trying to take it all in. *My very own bathroom as well, bet Albert hasn't got his own bathroom. Can't wait to tell him about this.*

"Is this all you've got?" she asks, emptying my haversack onto the bed. "Don't you have any other clothes?"

"No, that's all I have with me. Alan's got my other

clothes." "Who's Alan?"

"He's one of the lady's sons I was evacuated with before I came here. He's got my other pullover, my best trousers, and the new boots that my mother bought me."

"Why?"

"I don't know. His mother was always letting him wear my clothes."

She shakes her head and says, "When you've finished having your bath, come down to the kitchen for something to eat, OK?"

"Yes, OK."

After I've eaten, Mrs. Abelson introduces me to her husband. He's sitting in a wheelchair by the fire in a room they call a library. And although he's in a sitting position, it's very easy for me to tell he's a tall man. As I make my way over to his wheelchair to shake his outstretched hand, I notice a photograph of him on the piano. He's in the center of a small group of other Air Force men under the wing of an airplane. He looks a lot slimmer on the photo than he does now.

He closes his book and lays it on the table besides him. "Hello, Raymond, it's a pleasure to meet you. Take a seat." When I've shaken his hand, I sit in an armchair opposite. It's so big that my feet don't touch the floor. There are pictures and wooden models of airplanes everywhere, there's even one hanging from the ceiling. When I turn back to look at Mr. Abelson, I catch him looking down at my boots. I quickly pull myself forward so that my feet are flat on the carpet.

"Do you like airplanes Raymond?" he

asks. Yes," I say, "but not German ones."

"No, that's right," he says, laughing. "None of us like German ones do we?"

After talking for an hour or so, mostly about where I come from, and about my family, I ask him why he's in a wheelchair. I've been wanting to ask that question since I came into the room, but up until then, I hadn't had the courage to do it.

"It was a crash landing," he says. "After returning from a bombing session."

"A crash landing?"

"Yes, that's right. Jolly old wheels wouldn't come down. Next thing I know, I wake up in hospital to be told I'll never walk again. Damaged the old spine you see."

I feel very sorry and embarrassed for asking him such a question. I don't know what to say anymore. Just then the door opens and in walks Mrs. Abelson, carrying a plate of biscuits and a cup of cocoa.

"When you've finished eating, Raymond," she says. "You must go to bed. We have to be up early in the morning. We've lots to do tomorrow."

I'm curious as to know what she means by "we've lots to do tomorrow." *What about school?* I decide not to ask. That night I drift in and out of sleep, dreaming Mrs. Davis has come and taken me back to the Simmons' house. "It was only temporary," she keeps saying. "You were told that."

New Billet AND New Boots!

The next morning after breakfast . . .

"The first thing we have to do today, when I've finished here," Mrs. Abelson says, as she settles in front of her typewriter, "is to buy you some new clothes and a new pair of boots. I've got permission from Miss Grainger to keep you off school, so you don't have to worry about that."

The car, which has already been brought out of the garage, is sitting on the drive a few feet from the front door.

"Are we going in the car?" I ask, looking through the window.

"Yes," she says winding a new piece of paper into her typewriter. "We're going in the car, but don't get too impatient, I've got a lot of work to do first."

"OK, I'll just wait outside."

"You can sit inside the car if you want," she shouts, "as long as you don't touch anything, that is."

I race to the car after promising I won't touch anything. I sit myself down next to the driver's seat with my arms folded. After a while, I lean back with my hands behind my head imagining I'm driving the car and Mrs. Abelson is sitting next to me. I'm driving past our school, waving to all the kids with a big show-off smirk on my face.

When Mrs. Abelson finishes her typing, she dashes out of the house, around to the front of the car, and starts cranking the engine. After three or four unsuccessful turns of the starting handle, she straightens up, rubs her back, and then has another try. It still doesn't start, so she shouts for Nancy to sit with her foot on the accelerator. That does the trick, and the engine starts up. She jumps in, waves to her husband, and we move off. Once out of the driveway, she puts the speedometer up to 30, and we head for town.

A couple of miles further on, not too far from my school, she has to stop for the crossroads. My best friend Eddie is standing on the corner in the pouring rain, waiting to cross the street. He looks soaked to the skin. I'm desperate for him to see me in the car, so I jump up and kneel on the seat to attract his attention, but he doesn't turn around. I knock harder on the window. "Come on Eddie," I shout. "Please turn around."

"He can't hear you," Mrs. Abelson says as she blows the horn. "Not with the window up and his coat pulled over his head."

Eddie's head swivels round and looks straight at the car. I wave again. When he sees me, his mouth drops open and his eyes nearly pop out of his head. "I'm sorry," Mrs. Abelson says, as she presses the accelerator. "We can't stop here, we have to keep moving." As we drive away, I turn and wave through the back window. Eddie still doesn't wave, he just keeps standing there with his coat pulled over his head and a vacant look on his face. When he's out of sight, I twist around and settle down into the soft leather seat again.

When we get to the shops, she takes her and her husband's ration books out of her bag for the assistant to see if she has enough coupons for all my new clothes. There aren't any left in my ration book because Mrs. Simmons has used them all up. But it doesn't matter, there's enough as it turns out to buy me a new set of clothes, a new pair of boots, and even a snake belt, which I wasn't expecting. George, my eldest brother, was the only one out of my brothers who had a snake belt. I remember it quite clearly. It had red, white, and blue stripes along it. He saved his paper round pocket money up for weeks just to buy it. When Frank asked Mam for a snake belt, he was told that he'll just have to put up with wearing braces like all the others have to, there are more important things to spend money on than snake belts, young fella-me-lad.

Mrs. Abelson asks the assistant to throw my squishy boots and holey socks in the bin. "He doesn't need these boots anymore," she tells her. "They're much too far gone to be mended." When we get back in the car, she says, "We'll have to get plenty of polish on those boots when we get home, Raymond. You can hear them squeaking a mile off."

As soon as we get back, I go up to my bedroom and try all my new things on again before putting them away in the wardrobe. When I've done that, while I'm waiting for my tea, I sit in front of the window and look down at the old man cutting the lawns. It's stopped raining, so he can finish where he left off yesterday. I watch and marvel at the perfectly straight lines he's making. Then he moves out of sight to another part of the lawn and I can't see him anymore. I shade my eyes with my hand and spend the next few minutes looking out at the beautiful scenery. It's a clear sunny evening now, so I can see for miles, even as far as the mountains. It really is beautiful … I wish I could live here forever.

Tea won't be ready for another hour, so I lay on the bed reading a comic. Mrs. Simmons' face flashes before me again; it's always flashing before me. It makes me tense up. I've been trying to get her out of my mind ever since I arrived here, but I can't. I keep hearing her screaming voice, over and over again ... "You'll stay in there 'til you own up, you thieving little sod." It woke me up twice last night, dreaming about her. I dreamt I was back in that black hole under the stairs again.

I get up and go over to the window again. And as I stand there, I think about Miss Grainger telling Mrs. Davis about this being only temporary. Where will they put me when I do leave here? Will it be another house like the Simmons' house? I didn't want to go back to that kind of life again. I wanted to stay here with the Abelson's. I wanted to be free of the pain and indignity Mrs. Simmons put me through. *Please God, don't send me back to that life again.*

* * * * *

On a Sunday evening a couple of weeks later, I'm sat by the window in the conservatory when I notice somebody running across the field outside. I jump up to get a closer look. It's a boy, and he's being chased by a policeman. I put my boots on and run down to the fence to see what's going on. When I get there he's nowhere to be seen. I stand for ages, wondering where he could have possibly gone. It's like he suddenly disappeared into space.

After a while I make my way back toward the house, and as I step inside the conservatory to close the door, I hear someone shout. I look back to see the policeman standing in the field on the other side of the fence. He cups his hands round his mouth and shouts, "Did you see a boy come this way by any chance?" I'm about to tell him I did, then change my mind. "No," I shout. "I'm sorry, didn't see anything." I stand and watch him continue his search until he eventually gives up and disappears into the distance.

A few minutes later a voice calls from behind me. I turn

round and the boy steps out of the tool shed.

"How did you get in there?"

"I crawled under the fence and got inside just before you came out of the house. Thanks for telling him you didn't see me."

He's a tall, skinny kid, with a thick mop of ginger hair and a face full of freckles. He keeps looking round to see if the policeman has gone.

"It's all right," I say. "He's gone. Why was he chasing you?"

"He caught me walking along the railway embankment."

"I've been caught on there a few times myself," I tell him. "Taking a shortcut home."

"I wasn't taking a shortcut," he says. "I was just up there wondering how long it would take me to walk back to Liverpool."

I'd already deduced from his accent that he was an evacuee from Liverpool.

"Why? What's wrong with your billet, isn't it any good?"

"No, my billet's OK, it's just that I'm worried about my mother and baby sister back in Liverpool. The Germans have been bombing Liverpool every single night lately."

"How will you know the way?"

"Just by following the railway tracks."

"It's a long way," I tell him. "The train took ages to get here."

"I know, but it's the only way I can get there. I've got no money for train fares." He nods his head toward the house. "You're lucky staying in a place like that."

"I've only just moved in a couple of weeks ago."

"What are the people like?"

"They're nice people, better than the last ones. When are you thinking of going?"

"In the next few days if I don't get a letter from my mother, that is. Can't understand why she hasn't written. I always get a letter from her every week. She never misses."

"Is your dad in the Army then?"

"My dad's dead."

"What happened to him?"

"His ship got torpedoed. He was only in the Navy a few weeks."

"I'm sorry."

"That's another reason why I want to get home. I'm fourteen now, which means I can get a job and help look after Mam and my sister. Is your mother still in Liverpool?"

"No, she's here in Llanelli, but there's no room in the house for me. That's why I'm living here. I'll have to wait until the war's over before I can get back with her."

"That's if the Germans don't get here first."

The mere thought of the German Army taking over Liverpool, never mind stepping onto English soil, was beyond imagination. "Get here in this country? Do you really think they will?"

I hope not," he says. "But going by what I've read in the papers lately, it's looking very bad for us. Don't you read the papers?"

I'm about to tell him I only read comics when the sirens start sounding.

"I'll have to go," he says, "before the bombing starts."

"They'll let you stay in their air raid shelter if you want."

"No, it's OK. I'll be home in a few minutes. Might see you in Liverpool sometime."

There were no bombs dropped on Llanelli that night, but they did bomb Swansea again ... unmercifully.

* * * * *

A couple of weeks later I decide to go round to his billet. It's over a pub opposite the Dock Cinema. His landlady takes me inside and tells me he's gone back to Liverpool.

"When?" I ask. "Last week," she says. "His uncle came and got him. It was terrible. His mother's house got a direct hit during one of the bombing raids; killed her and his baby sister."

It was during the first week of May 1941 that his mother's house got bombed. The week that later became known as the "May Blitz," the week that Liverpool suffered its worst bombings. May 1, 1941, would go down in history as the first of seven consecutive harrowing nights of the heaviest bombings that the people of Liverpool would endure throughout the six years of the war. The word "blitz," incidentally (which I found out just recently), comes from the word "blitzkrieg," an abbreviation of Hitler's threatened lightning war.

When the sirens rang out at around 10:30 p.m. on that first night of May, mothers everywhere jumped out of their beds, grabbed their children, and dashed for the safety of an air raid shelter. By now they were getting used to the routine of spending another six or seven hours in air raid shelters, after all, they'd been doing it for over a year. But what they didn't know was that this particular night was to be quite different from any of the other nights.

Train Track To Liverpool

My mother had unwittingly arranged a week's visit to Liverpool that very same week. The reason for the visit was to see her mother; my grandfather, a publican, had died when my mother was just three years old. She and two of my sisters, Muriel and Dorothy, arrived in Liverpool on Thursday afternoon, the first of May. And because it had been arranged for them to stay with Dad's parents, Uncle Harold, Dad's brother, met them at Edge Hill Station, about a mile from my grandparents' house.

Uncle Harold was the youngest and the only one of Dad's four brothers (he didn't have any sisters) that was still single. Forever the city slicker was Uncle Harold, in his white shirt and armbands. He was always dressed like he was going to a wedding, the ultimate in Dandyism as you might say. He had an eye for the women, too, and because of his many little money-making rackets, he was never short of a few shillings to spend on his lady friends. He was a nice guy. I met him for the first time after the war, when Frank and I had to stay in Grandad's house until Mam could afford some extra beds.

When they stepped into the street from the station, they were staggered at the devastation that lay before them. My mother knew by what she'd read in the papers that Liverpool had had more than its fair share of the bombings, but she didn't expect anything like this. The Germans, she thought, have been more than busy. Practically every street between Grandma's street and the station had been bombed. The sight of people ravaging through the mountains of bricks and rubble brought tears to her eyes. As they passed St. Mary's church, she noticed that Gerry had managed to drop a bomb on that as well, the church that Dad and her had got married in eighteen years earlier.

Nin (my grandmother) had a nice hot dinner waiting for them all. Grandad, as per usual, was still in the pub. Mam would have been very surprised if he had met them at the station. She knew what he was like; he was never out of the pub. He'd stay there until he was literally chucked out. Dad didn't like his father; in fact, he hated him with a vengeance. Grandad had scarred his memory with the beatings he'd bestowed on him and his four brothers. He even beat poor little Nin. Dad said he would never forgive him for beating his mother, and he didn't, even right up to his dying day.

Grandad had never done a day's work since he absconded from the Royal Navy in his early twenties. Why the authorities never caught up with him, I'll never know. He had three pastimes my Grandad ... sleeping, smoking, and drinking beer. When he wasn't in the pub, he'd spend the rest of the time sitting by the fire with his nose in the paper or listening to the wireless.

He possessed no self-pride whatsoever. It didn't bother him to have to rely on his wife to put food on the table, or clothing on her or their children's backs. And because there wasn't enough money to buy shoes, for a long time Dad and his four brothers had to go to school in their bare feet. Years later, after Grandad's death, Dad often said that his father was the laziest and meanest man God ever put breath to.

* * * * *

The piercing noise of the sirens suddenly started around 10:30 p.m. Mam and Muriel were sitting by the fire with Nin and Uncle Harold. Mam dashed upstairs and pulled Dorothy from her bed and retreated to the cellar with everyone else. They huddled under a steel table; Nin said they'd be much safer under there.

It was a reinforced metal table called a Morrison Shelter, named after its inventor, Herbert Morrison, a member of Parliament at the time. They saved many lives, especially for those who couldn't get to an air raid shelter. They never built an air raid shelter in Nin's street simply because the street was too narrow. The authorities said the shelter would have prevented any traffic getting through, such as the fire brigade and the ambulances.

In later years Mam told us that she never expected to get out of that basement alive. It was the most terrifying experience anyone could endure she said. One of the explosions shook the house so badly that it brought some heavy chunks of ceiling plaster crashing down on top of the steel table, but they weren't hurt. Muriel was crying all the time and praying for the planes to go away. The bombing just went on and on, hour after hour. They could hear people screaming outside. Uncle Harold said he thought one of the houses close by might have been hit, but Nin wouldn't let him go and look; it's too dangerous, she said, stay under the table.

Six or seven hours later, as dawn started to break, the bombing suddenly stopped. Then the sounds of ambulances and fire engines began as they raced up and down the streets. Nin put her hands together and thanked God that they were all still alive. They were all covered in a white dust from the ceiling; it was even in their eyes and mouths.

After being crouched under the table for so long, they could hardly walk up the cellar stairs. Granddad was still in his chair in the kitchen—he hadn't moved all night, except to make a cup of tea and make some toast in front of the fire. "Why didn't you come down in the cellar?" Nan asked. "You'd have been a lot safer there." "If Adolph f*&#$%g Hitler wants me dead," Grandad said. "He'll have to come over to England and shoot me himself."

Uncle Harold opened the front door to look outside. At first he couldn't believe what he was seeing. All he saw was a giant pyramid of bricks on the other side of the road where two houses once stood.

Firemen and policemen were tearing at the bricks and rubble with their bare hands, so were the neighbors. Uncle Harold had known those people all his life, he'd grown up with their kids, gone to the same school. He ran over to help, but it was no use. The policeman told him there was very little chance of anyone getting out alive, the two houses had had a direct hit.

Mam was too frightened to stay after the fourth day, so as soon as they were able to get a train she packed their bags and beat a hasty retreat back to South Wales.

* * * * *

They were nice, genuine, good-hearted people, the Abelson's; they couldn't do enough for me. Each evening after tea, Mr. Abelson would help me with my homework. "Come on, Raymond," he'd say. "I'll make you the top of your class before we're finished." And in all the time I lived there, I never once had to walk home from school in the rain. The arrangement was that when it was raining, I'd shelter in the vestry doorway until Mrs.

Abelson came to pick me up. I used to wish it would rain every day because I loved riding in her car. But unfortunately it all came to an abrupt end. Miss Grainger certainly wasn't exaggerating when she said it would only be a temporary stay.

Just eight short weeks, and here I am once more with nowhere to live. And what's worse, I never said goodbye to Mr. and Mrs. Abelson last night. I should have at least waited until they got up this morning. I wanted to, but I was still upset after what she 'd told me.

"Raymond, Mrs. Davis is coming tomorrow to take you to a new billet. I'm so sorry to have to do this at such short notice. I wanted to tell you a week ago, but I couldn't pluck up the courage. You did know that your stay here was only a temporary one, didn't you? We've sold the house, you see, we're going to live in America." I was devastated.

I'd been walking along the railway tracks for about an hour. My intentions once I arrived at the next station were to sneak a ride on the first train back to Liverpool. I wasn't sure whether I'd get away with it, but I wanted to try. I planned to go to my Nin's house and stay with her until the war was over. But the further along I got and the more I thought about it, it began to look like a very bad idea. I stopped and sat down alongside the railway lines.

For a start, I don't know where they live, and even if I do find them, from what I've heard of how bad tempered and grouchy Granddad is all the time, there's a good chance he'll tell me to sod off back to South Wales.

I stood up, turned round, and headed back to the school.

Mrs. Abelson's car is outside—she's just about to drive away when she sees me. She gets out, runs over, and puts her arms around me in a rib-crushing hug. Tears leak down her face. I tell her I'm very sorry for running away. "Doesn't matter," she says.

"I understand."

Her husband calls me over to the car, puts his hand out of the window to shake mine, and gives me half-a-crown (a considerable amount of money in those days, enough to get me in the Saturday matinee for the next twelve weeks). "Don't worry," he says. "The war will be over soon, and then you'll be able to go back with your family again." I stand and wave as they drive off, swallowing hard, and soaking the tears up with my sleeve. Once their car turns the corner out of sight, I walk through the playground and into the classroom. When I sit down behind my desk, I have a terrible empty feeling in my stomach. I know that deep down, as much as I'd really like to, I'll probably never ever see them again.

I open my desk to get my pen and exercise book. There's a parcel inside. It says "To Raymond, from Mr. and Mrs. Abelson." I look up at Miss Grainger to see if it's OK to open it. She nods a yes. There's a new pair of pants inside, and a pullover, and a brand new pair of boots. One of the boots has an envelope sticking out of it with a letter inside.

Dear Raymond,

We are so sorry it had to come to this, but we had no alternative, we have to move to America to live. Someday, when you are older, you will under- stand. We've enjoyed having you stay with us, and hope someday, when the war is over, we might meet up again. Until then, God be with you.

All our love ...
Rachel and Simon Abelson

I had that letter in my possession for many years, right up

until 1995, as a matter of fact. It went missing during our move from the UK to America.

Being Jewish and the constant fear of imminent occupation by the Germans was the reason for the Abelson's quick departure from Britain to the U.S.

Penalty For Stealing A Pork Pie

In June 1942, I'm taken to my new billet—my fifth. I wasn't aware of it at the time, but Mrs. Abelson had already arranged everything with Mrs. Davis about a week before they left. My new landlady is a close friend of the Abelson's. As a matter of fact, I'd seen her in the Abelson's house on a couple of occasions.

Over two and a half years have passed since I was separated from my mother. But wanting to be back with her just doesn't seem to be important any more. I don't know why, but I've began to think that my mother might have started to feel she'd be a lot better off without me. Maybe she's got used to not having all the work and worry of bringing up so many kids now. Anyway, I gave up caring about it a long time ago; I have no real tears in me anymore. At eight and a half years of age, to cover my bashfulness and insecurity I pretend to be streetwise and cocksure of myself. And it works most of the time, except that on some occasions it gets me involved in fights in the schoolyard and in trouble with the teachers.

Just recently my mother has complained to Mrs. Davis that my visits over the past year are getting fewer and fewer, and by moving me even further away, it may stop me from visiting her altogether. Mrs. Davis told Mam that because the bombings over Liverpool have worsened, it's bringing in more evacuees than ever, consequently making it considerably more difficult to find billets for everyone. But as soon as she can arrange it, she will try to move me closer.

Mrs. Jenkins has two children, Gareth, who works for Thompson's, the butcher somewhere downtown, and Shirley, who's just started her first year in school. I liked the Jenkins family straight away. Mrs. Jenkins, who is a slim, attractive lady in her middle to late thirties, makes me very welcome. And Gareth, who is sixteen, thinks it's a great idea of his mother's to take in an evacuee. He has no qualms about moving into his sister's bedroom so I can have his, he told her. "Gareth's a good boy," his mother says. "He often helps around the house when I'm not well." And since his father's job move six months earlier to a munitions factory up north, she's become even more proud of her eldest son, especially the way he looks after her and little Shirley.

Before her husband boarded the Sheffield-bound train the night he was leaving, and because he was concerned about his wife's health, he took Gareth to one side and asked him to take good care of his mother and sister while he was away. Gareth hugged his father and promised he would, and told him not to worry about them. He told his dad he could rely on him one hundred percent. He was a nice, kind, thoughtful person, Gareth Jenkins, a person whom I quickly became very fond of.

On Sunday afternoons I enjoyed many an hour in the garden shed watching him make cigarette lighters out of spent rifle shells his uncle brought him from his Home Guard training. He seemed to be able to put his hand to anything. It wasn't a bad little businesin one single afternoon he could easily turn out at least four lighters. Sixpence each he sold them for, quite easily as a matter of fact; plenty of people smoked around there.

In the summer evenings when I was on school holiday, he'd take me on the bus to Pewll Sands where I'd sit on the beach watching him catch crabs. He'd roll his trousers up and paddle through the miniature lakes that were left from the outgoing tide. Then, bending down until his nose nearly touched the water, he'd scrape the bottom with a stick to disturb any crabs that might be hiding. Once he saw one, he'd plunge his hand down and grab it. "What do you think of that one Raymond?" he'd shout, holding it up in the air like it was some sort of a trophy. "Bet that's worth sixpence of anyone's money." I'd never seen crabs so big—they were enormous, some of them larger than a dinner plate. He carried them home in a big sack and sold them round the street to neighbors and friends.

Gareth even let me play records on his wind-up gramophone.

One evening, he comes in from work and asks me if I'd be interested in working in the butcher's shop on Saturdays.

"What do I have to do?"

"It's easy," he says. "All you have to do is brush up every now and again, and make a cup of tea for anybody that wants one."

"How much do I get for that?" "Nine pence."

"Nine pence? Wow. How long do I have to work?"
"A couple of hours, that's all"

"Nine pence? Just for a couple of hours work?" "Yes."

"When do I start?"

"Next Saturday morning at ten o'clock."

It's only Monday, and yet suddenly next Saturday seems a lifetime away.

That night, before I go to sleep, I sit up thinking about all the different things I can buy with my first Saturday's wages.

When Tuesday comes, I go into Woolworth's on my way home from school to see if there's anything in the store that might take my fancy. I'm always walking round "Woolie's," looking at things I can't afford. But this time it's going to be different, this time I've got money of my own, and a whole nine pence at that.

I go from counter to counter looking at all sorts, but everything I like costs nearly twice as much as my nine pence. Then, just as I'm on my way out, I see on a shelf behind a counter a Gene Autry cowboy gun and holster. I stop and goggle at it with my mouth open. The gun is silver, just like Gene's, and the belt, which is loaded with lots of pretend bullets, has a big silver buckle with the initials G.A. across it. *A Gene Autry gun and holster, I wonder how much that is?*

The girl behind the counter sees me staring at it.

"It's two shillings and eleven pence," she says. "Do you want it?"

"No" I say, walking away. "I don't have any money."

But when I get halfway to the door I get an idea and run back to the counter. "Do you put things away if you put a deposit on them?"

"Yes, how much do you want to put down?"

"I don't have money until Saturday. Can you put it under the counter until then."

"Until Saturday? No I can't, not unless you put a deposit on it first."

"Is it the only one you have? Do you have any more?"

"No, we don't have any more. It is the only one we have left. Now will you go away, I'm busy."

Thinking she might feel sorry for me and change her mind, I put an angelic look on my face and ask her, "Do you think it might be sold by Saturday? I really like it you see."

She leans over the counter, "How the hell should I know if it'll be sold by Saturday? Now will you bugger off, I'm BUSY."

Every day from the Tuesday to the following Friday, before I go home, I run round to Woolie's with my fingers crossed to check if the Gene Autry gun and holster is still on the shelf.

When Saturday morning comes along, the morning I'm to start my new job, I decide to leave the house a little earlier to allow me enough time to go into Woolie's and check one last time. It's still there, where it's always been, hanging from the display behind the counter. I dash out of the store, and down the street to the shop. *Just another two hours, and it'll be mine.*

When I walk into the butcher's and look around, who do I see behind the counter but the man I'd stolen the pie from, he's standing right next to Gareth. *Oh shit, not him. What's he doing here? He must own two shops.*

I'm just about to make a run for it when he glances over, looks at me for a second, then turns away and carries on cutting meat. My heart missed a beat. I thought he'd recognized me. I'm trying my best to get rid of the guilty look on my face when Gareth comes over and takes me into the back of the shop.

While he's showing me what to do, the rear door opens and in walks the delivery boy, just arriving back from one of his deliveries. He nods and says hello. I say hello back then continue to listen to my instructions from Gareth. When Gareth goes back into the shop, the unthinkable happens—the delivery boy suddenly recognizes me. He taps me on the shoulder, grabs me by my collar, and says, "It was you that stole the pie that day, wasn't it? You bloody little thief."

I don't say anything, just stare at him with a guilty look on my face.

"I thought I'd seen you somewhere before when I first came in. You just wait there while I call Mr. Thompson." While he's opening the door to the shop to tell his boss, I grab my coat from the hook and make a quick departure by way of the rear door. When I get out into the street I hear him shouting, "MR. THOMPSON, I'VE GOT THE BOY THAT STOLE THE PIE."

I don't stop running until I get to the house. Mrs. Jenkins is on the front step talking to a neighbor, so I run around the back, up the stairs, and into my bedroom. I sit on the bed crying, my head in a turmoil.

How can I face Mrs. Jenkins when she finds out what I've done? And what about Garath, and Mrs. Davis, and Miss Grainger, what' are they going to think? No one will ever trust me again. They'll put me in that home this time, I know they will. I wish I was dead.

There's a knock on the door. Mrs. Jenkins has seen me running around the back.

"Raymond, are you in

there?" "Yes, Mrs. Jenkins."

She opens the door and pops her head round. "What's the matter? Why are you crying?"

"I'm sorry Mrs. Jenkins," I say. "I'm really

sorry." "Sorry? Sorry for what Raymond?"

I don't know how to begin to tell her. I just keep shaking my head. Just then the front door opens. It's Gareth. He shouts upstairs for his mother. She goes down wondering why he's home so early. "That's funny," she says. "Gareth home so early, the shop doesn't close 'til one o'clock on Saturdays."

I get up from the bed and open the door so I can hear what they're saying. But because the kitchen door is closed, it's only bits of muffled conversation I can hear; which is mainly from his mother. "Stole a pie?" "Are you sure?" "Mary Simmons, the school teacher?" "When did this all happen?"

I was thoroughly confused as I tried to fathom out what they were saying ... Mary and Mrs. Simmons? What have they got to do with it?

When they finish talking, they both come up to my bedroom. Mrs. Jenkins comes over to the bed. "It's alright, Raymond," she says. "The butcher has forgiven you for stealing his pie."

"Forgiven me?"

"Yes" she says. "And if you still want to work there, it's OK
with him."

"Why has he forgiven me?"

"Mary Simmons told him all about it."

I'm still confused as to how Mary came to be involved in it. "How does Mary know?" I ask.

"She was in the queue outside when you walked into the shop," Mrs. Jenkins says. "Mary gets her meat from there every Saturday morning."

Mary had told the butcher all about her stepmother separating my food rations from the rest of the family's.

RE Loves SJ

The Cost Of A Kiss

One Sunday afternoon, shortly after I've moved in, Terry, a boy from next door, and three other boys, Alfie, Llew (short

for Llewellyn), and Dai (sounds like die when spoken, a Welsh nickname for David) call at the house to ask if I want to join their gang. After I tell them I'd be more than happy to join, I'm taken to Terry's dad's garden shed to be properly introduced to every- one; that's where all their meetings are always held.

Because of his size, Llew, who's nine, could easily be taken for a fourteen year old. He's a big, chubby, red-faced kid, who most of the time wears a permanent scowl on his face. None of the other kids' mothers likes their children playing with Llew, especially Alfie's mother. Every time Alfie is leaving the house to go out to play, she peers through the parlor window to see if big

Llew is in the street. If he is, she'll say to little Alfie, "I don't know why you would want to play with that Llew Griffiths, he's just like his father, he'll come to no good you know."

Alfie is only half way through telling me all about himself when Llew comes over and pushes in front of him. "I'm going to be a rugby player when I grew up, you know," he says. This interruption annoys Alfie, but he doesn't say anything, he's used to Llew doing that. He does it to everyone.

"Are you?" I say, trying to convince him I'm

interested. "Yes," Llew replies.

Then, turning to the others for their full agreement, says, "Sright, in-it?"

Everyone nods—they have to. Personally I couldn't have cared less if big Llew, in the course of time, turned out to be a coal man, but because I have no desire to get my nose flattened, I say, "Cor, that's fantastic. You'll be famous one day then?"

"Yep. My dad's told me I'll be good enough to play for Llanelli when I grow up. That's why I've got to start training now while I'm young."

"Where do you train?" Alfie asks.

Llew looks down at Alfie, shakes his head, and says, "I

wasn't talking to you."

"I'm sorry," Alfie says. "I was only asking, that's all. I didn't know you were training to be a rugby player."

You can tell by the look on Llew's face that he's fast losing patience with Alfie. "Where do you think I train?" Llew asks. making the question sound irrelevant. "I train on Llanelli's rugby ground, of course, with all the other rugby players."

Alfie doesn't believe a word he's saying, and neither does anyone else. He knows all too well he's telling lies just like the rest of the gang does. "How many times a week?" Alfie asks.

Llew blows another agitated sigh. "Three, times a week, what do you think?"

"Three times a week?" Alfie repeats. "Wow. Can we come and watch?"

For a few seconds Llew has to think how he's going to answer that question. "No," he says. "They don't allow any spectators when we're training."

Llew was lying through his teeth, of course—the only time he'd seen the inside of Llanelli's rugby ground was on Saturday afternoons when he sneaked a peek through the hole in the fence.

* * * * *

Alfie is quite small for his age, so small in fact that his clothes always look three sizes too big for him. For instance, his pants, because they fall past his knees onto his shins, makes him look like he's wearing long pants. And because his clothes are hand-me-downs, practically everything he wears is covered in patches. The patches wouldn't be half as noticeable if his mother used a similar colored material for each patch, but unfortunately for him she doesn't.

His mother works behind the counter in a shop on Station Road that sells newspapers, sweets, and tobacco. And because of that, just recently she's been able to get Alfie a job delivering the morning newspapers for Mr. Philpot, her boss. Mr. Philpot first thought Alfie was a little small to lug a big bag of newspapers around, but because his mother has been working there for so long, he feels obliged to give her son a try.

But as small as Alfie is, he has no trouble delivering the papers. In fact, he always gets back to the shop half an hour earlier than the previous delivery boy used to. That makes his mother very proud of him. And it's not only Alfie's mother that likes him working in the sweet shop, the rest of the gang does as well, and for a good reason I might add.

Alfie had only been working there about a week when he asked Terry if he could arrange for him and the rest of the gang to meet up in the shed every Saturday when he'd finished his paper round. Terry, of course, didn't hesitate to agree when he found out why. The idea of the get-together was for Alfie to share the bag of Hollands Treacle Toffees Mr. Philpots gave him every Saturday. The first time they saw the toffee their eyes were popping out of their heads. "Cor, treacle toffee, haven't had that since before the war." "It's for being a good delivery boy," Alfie told them.

The shame of it all was that the weekly gatherings for free treacle toffee were only to last for a few short weeks. The disappointment on everyone's face when Alfie entered the shed empty handed that Saturday afternoon was a sorry sight to behold. But that wasn't the only problem—Alfie had lost his job and so had his mother. She'd been a reliable and trustworthy employee for Mr. Philpot for the best part of five years, but who could blame Mr. Philpot for terminating Alfie and his mother. After all, as Mr. Philpot told Alfie's mother that day, "Alfie wasn't satisfied with the piece of toffee I gave him every Saturday. Oh no, he has to get greedy and steal a whole bar of toffee. I'm sorry Mrs. Mathews, but if every employee were stealing toffee at the rate your son is, I'd be bankrupt in no time."

* * * * *

Every time little Alfie tries to get involved in any conversation, Llew gives him a shove and tells him to shurrup and be quiet. I feel sorry for Alfie when Llew does that. Alfie is in fact a sharp, brainy little kid. He can even say his nine times-table right through without even making one single mistake.

The trouble with Alfie is he doesn't realize that Llew (who only possesses half a brain) is extremely jealous and envious of his frequent intelligent suggestions.

Dai, one of the other members of the gang, is the youngest, and because he always wipes his nose on his balaclava, or if it happens to be in the summertime, on his sleeve, he's called "Dai Snot." His nose is always running, no matter what time of day it is; makes me feel sick just looking at him. Constantly worried of him catching a cold, his mother always insists he wear his balaclava when playing out. And to keep his chest warm, she even makes him wear all his pullovers back to front, even in the summer.

Llew has always insisted on being the leader, ever since the gang was first formed. But because Terry's dad lets the gang have the use of his shed for their meetings, and the fact that Llew's dad can't afford a shed (because he only has a part-time job), Llew always loses the vote by a very large majority. Llew hates being second in command. Not a day passes by without him reminding everyone that the day his dad does get a shed will be the day that he'll expect to procure his rightful position.

Llew's told everyone his dad is one of the grounds men at the rugby ground, which is another lie. The reason he hasn't gone into the Army like all the other kids' dads isn't because he's scared of getting shot (like some of the kids are always saying to him), it's just that he has one leg shorter than the other—or so he says.

Before we leave the house to go to the shed, Dai Snot, who's sitting on his go-cart, looks up and asks me if I wouldn't mind pushing him round to Terry's house. The go-cart consists of two planks of wood and four pram wheels his father has put together for him. Dai steers the go-cart with two pieces of string that are tied to the front axle. When I bend down and put my hands on his shoulders to start pushing him, Llew says, "I wouldn't push him, if I were you."

"Why?"

"Cause if you do, he'll always want you to push him. He's a lazy little sod, he never walks anywhere."

But I do push Dai because he's promised he'll let me have a go of his cart after the meeting is over. And he does, just like he promised he would. He lets me ride it down Begin Hill. "That's the best place," Dai says. "It really goes fast down there." Fast is an understatement—I speed down Begin Hill at speeds Ben Hur would have been proud of. And only for the fact that I tip over just before I reach the bottom did I not finish up inside Austin's chandlery shop.

When we get to the shed we all sit in a circle on wooden boxes. Then Terry takes the rules list down from the back of the door and gives them to me to read. It's only one page, so it does- n't take me long. When I've finished reading the rules, Llew takes them from me and pins them back on the door.

"You haven't finished yet," he says. "You've one more thing to do before you can become a proper member."

"What's that?" I ask.

"You have to kiss Sally Jackson. Once you've done that, then you're a proper member of the gang."

"Kiss Sally Jackson?" I ask, thinking it must be some sort of joke they're having with me. "Why?"

"Because it's one of the rules," Llew says. "That's why."

"And you have to do it while we're all watching," Terry says.

I'm sat on the box totally confused and wondering why kissing some girl (whoever she may be) has to be one of their rules.

"All the other boys round here are scared to kiss her," Llew says. "And it's not because she's ugly or anything, it's because she's really pretty. So we want to know if you've got the guts to do it. If you have, you're in the gang. If you haven't got the guts to do it, then you're not in the gang."

"What if she doesn't want to kiss me?"

"She will," Llew says. "She likes kissing boys."

"She's not half pretty," Alfie says. "Wait till you see

her." "Shurrup," Llew says. "We're doing the talking."

I'm starting to get quite nervous, because the only other female I've kissed up until now in my young life is my mother.

"We've all done it," Llew says boastfully. "Don't worry about it."

"Not all of us," Alfie says, rolling his eyes toward Dai

Snot. "Well, what do you think?" Llew asks. "Do you want to or not?"

I'm in a quandary, I want to say no and go home, but I also want to join the gang. "I don't even know Sally Jackson," I say, as if it really matters.

"Doesn't matter," Terry says. "She's my cousin."

"And it has to be on the lips," Llew says, poking his stubby finger into my chest. "Not on the cheek."

"And we have to watch to make sure you do it, that's part of the rules," Alfie chips in.

"Will yer shurrup Alfie," Llew says. "We know what to tell im—he already knows that."

"Haven't you ever kissed a girl before?" Llew asks.

Thinking that they'd all had ample experience at kissing girls, at first I wasn't sure whether to tell the truth or not. "Ere, no, but I nearly did once."

"It's easy," Terry says. "Don't worry about it."

"Do I have to kiss her today," I ask, trying my best to squirm out of it, "or would tomorrow be OK?"

"Today," they all chorus. "Or you can't join the

gang." "What if I join tomorrow?"

"Look," Llew says. "We've already told you once, if you can't join now, you'll never be able to join. Which means you won't be able to play with us ever again."

"Well," Terry says, getting impatient. "Wharra about it?"

"He's scared," Llew scowls. "I can tell by his face. I knew he would be. Let's forget it."

"OK, OK," I say. "I'll do it."

Terry jumps up from his box. "Good," he says. "I'll go and get Sally."

After about ten or fifteen minutes, I get up and look through the window to see if they're coming, but there's no sign of either of them.

Llew can see by my face that I'm losing my nerve. So he gets up from his box, goes over to the door, folds his arms, and leans on it. "She'll be here in a minute," he says. "She's probably finishing her tea or something."

Then, after a few more agonizing minutes, Terry finally appears. But Sally is not with him. *Oh great, she's not coming.*

Trying my best not to show the great sense of relief that's

suddenly crept over me, I put a disappointed look on my face and ask Terry why she's decided not to come. "Don't worry," he says. "She is coming. She's on the toilet; she'll be here in a few minutes."

I sit back down on the box again, the great sense of relief that came over me a moment ago has now disappeared.

Eventually, after another long wait, Sally makes her appearance.

"About time," Llew blurts out. "We all thought you had fell down."

Sally, on hearing that, does no more but turn and run back to her house, her face as red as a beetroot.

"Why did you say that?" Terry asks.

"It was just a joke," Llew says. "Can't she take a joke?"

"She mightn't do it now," Alfie says. "You've embarrassed her." "She will," Llew says. "Go after her, Terry, she'll come back." Terry, after another long wait, manages to talk Sally around
and brings her back.

"This is Sally," he says. "She's my cousin."

Sally smiles and says hello. I blush and try to say hello back, but nothing comes out.

"OK," Terry says. "We'll go outside and wait."

They go outside and position themselves in front of the window, noses pressed against the glass. *I wish they'd go away. It's bad enough having to do this without them goggling at me.*

"Come on then," Sally says, closing her eyes and puckering

her lips. "You have to come closer if you want to kiss me."

I wipe my sleeve across my mouth and tentatively edge a little closer. Then without warning, she suddenly puts her arms around my neck, pulls me against her, and presses her lips hard against mine.

After about a very long ten seconds, I have to push her away. First to get my breath, and second, she's pressing so hard it's making my front teeth ache.

"What's the matter," she asks. "Didn't you like kissing

me?" "Yes," I say, gasping for air. "But I couldn't breathe."

She opens the shed door to go out. "You're supposed to breathe through your nose when you're kissing, stupid, not through your mouth."

Outside, I'm given a congratulatory slap on the back from everyone, and told I am now a fully bonafide member of the gang. I pretend there's nothing to it.

* * * * *

On my way home from school the next day I come upon two of Sally's friends in the street. One of them is playing hopscotch, while the other is busy chalking on everything that she can possibly find (including all over the wall of our house), "R.E. loves S.J."

I run into the house and grab the floor cloth from under the sink, dash back out, and begin rubbing it off the wall before my landlady sees it. And while I'm doing that they keep telling me that it won't make the slightest bit of difference how much I rub off, because by the time I go to school tomorrow everyone will already know all about it anyway. They say that when they were passing my school on their way home today they stopped at the gates and told everyone about Sally Jackson kissing the evacuee from Liverpool in Terry's dad's garden shed. And as I rub the chalk off the wall, the other girl is walking behind me writing on it again. In my temper, I grab the chalk off her and chase them both away from the house.

And as I continue to rub, I can't stop thinking about what it's going to be like having to go to school tomorrow and listen to everyone shouting "Raymond Evans loves Sally Jackson," and "Raymond Evans is a sissy."

Then the girl who I've taken the chalk from shouts from the bottom of the street, "You're in big trouble now Raymond Evans, Sally Jackson is going to have a baby."

I jump up and run after her. "A baby? What do you mean she's going to have a baby?"

"You should know why, you're the one that kissed her." At this point I'm not completely sure whether she's just kidding me, or whether it is in fact possible for a girl to have a baby after being kissed by a boy.

"I don't believe you. A girl can't have a baby just because she's been kissed by a boy."

"She can," she says. "If she's kissed for a very long time like you did."

"It's not true, is it?" I ask, hoping she'll put me out of my misery and tell me she really is only kidding.

"It is true," the other girl says. "You ask anyone."

I'm about to become a father and I'm only nine years old.

I don't want to listen to them any longer, so I race back up the street and bang on Sally's front door. Her mother opens it.

"Is Sally in?"

"She's not home from school yet."

I walk back to my billet. I'm out of my mind with worry. A few minutes later, Sally appears. I run up to her before she reaches her door.

"Is it true you're going to have a baby?"

She gives me a quizzical look and laughs. "Who told you that?" she asks. "Of course I'm not, silly."

"One of the girls from your school, she told me."

"Take no notice of her. Kissing doesn't give girls babies. She's just jealous because she's never been kissed by a boy before."

From Heartache

With My Haversack

To Home Haven

Sometime around the end of 1942 my father came home on a short weekend leave to give my mother the bad news she'd always dreaded. He'd been given a posting to a Royal Air Force base in Aden in the Middle East. Dad had the option of spending most of his embarkation leave in Llanelli and the remaining few days in Liverpool where he was to sail from. But wanting to say goodbye to his parents in Liverpool before he left, and the bomb- ing had eased off temporarily, he asked my mother if she would go with him to Liverpool for the whole of the two weeks. Mam agreed and took Stanley, Dorothy, and Edith with her while her landlady agreed to look after David, the baby. Dad's ship sailed out two weeks later, and Mam returned to Llanelli.

* * * * *

Three more months have passed by, and life before evacuation has become a distant memory. I'm enjoying my childhood again. I have nice clothes to go to school in. No more days of going to bed hungry, and even the relentless taunting has stopped. Things couldn't be better, or so I thought at the time.

It all happens on a Saturday afternoon as I sit on the cobbler's step putting my newly mended boots on. Mr. Jenkins has put extra studs in so they will last longer. He didn't charge me; he put them in for nothing. I should have waited until I'd got home before I put them on because I'm blocking his doorway stopping his customers from coming in. But because it's the first time I've had studs put in my boots, I can't wait until I get home.

While I'm in the middle of tying my laces Alfie comes by and tells me there's an ambulance in our street, and it's outside my house. When I've finished tying my laces, I get up and run home as fast as I can. I arrive just in time to see Mrs. Jenkins' mother getting into the back of the ambulance. I go over to Garath, who's standing on the step. He has tears streaming down his face.

"Who's in the ambulance?" I ask.

"It's my mum," he says in a broken voice. "She's very

ill." My eyes fill up. "Will she be all right?"

"I don't know," he says. "All I know is that the doctor's told me she's very ill and she's got to go in hospital right away."

The following week Mrs. Davis arrives at the house to tell me she'll collect me at nine o'clock in the morning to take me to my new billet. I already knew about it because Gareth's father, who'd arrived home the day after his wife had been taken away, had told me last night. He told me his wife was going to be in hospital for a very long time, and that he had no alternative but to have me moved to a new billet.

Before Gareth leaves for work the next morning he comes into my bedroom and tells me how much he's enjoyed having me around. He makes me promise him that when I move back to Liverpool after the war, I won't forget him and his family, and if I can, to come back and see them some day. He gets up from the bed, and hands me a bag of licorice sticks. "There's something for you to chew on your way," he says. "I know they're your favorites."

The next morning I'm leaning on the front gate talking to Terry and the gang when I see Mrs. Davis coming up the street. "You can still be a member," he says. "Which means you can come round anytime and play with us." It doesn't seem like a whole year has passed since he first knocked on the door and invited me to join. I thank him and tell him I will. Then Mrs. Davis arrives and asks me if I'm ready.

I go up the steps, push the front door open, and shout down the lobby to Gareth's grandmother that I'm going. She comes to the door and gives me a sixpence and tells me to keep in touch. I sling my gas mask and haversack over my shoulder and tell Mrs. Davis that I'm ready. I want to get away before Terry and the others notice the tears welling up in my eyes. After we've got to the bottom of the street, and I've waved to Terry, and Alfie, and big Llew, I ask Mrs. Davis where my new billet is.

"Number six Penry Place," she says. "You'll like this family; they're very nice people." I don't say anything, just nod my head and hope it won't be anything like the Simmons'.

After being lucky enough to live with people such as the Abelsons and the Jenkins family over the past ten months, I can't help feeling that things are about to turn for the worse. Will I be lucky enough to get three good billets on the trot?

Penry Place is a little cul-de-sac of about twenty houses. Number six is a three bedroom, terraced house that sits in the far left corner of the street. I'm feeling somewhat bewildered and a little wary as we approach the house. All the old feelings are coming back, and I'm wondering if my new landlady is going to be another Mrs. Jones or another Mrs. Simmons. Just like always, my stomach starts to quiver and I think I'm going to be sick.

I'll run away in the morning if she doesn't like me. Mrs. Davis will just have to find me somewhere else to live. I don't care.

Mrs. Williams is standing on her step talking to a group of neighbors. She's a small, slim lady in her late forties or maybe her early fifties, I can't remember. She wears glasses and has a kind looking face. After she shakes hands with the billeting officer, she stoops down and takes hold of my hand and squeezes it. "Hello Raymond," she says, in her beautiful, lilting Welsh accent. "How are you then?"

All the anxiety and uncertainty that has built up inside me disappears in an instant. My new landlady is a warm, tender, passionate woman, who has welcomed me into her house, not as an evacuee, but as a long lost son. She's so excited about taking me in that, once Mrs. Davis has left, she takes me round to practically every house on the street and introduces me to the rest of her neighbors. And they're all nice people as well, every single one of them. They don't even mention the word evacuee. "This is Raymond," Mrs. Williams says. "He's come all the way from Liverpool, and he's going to stay with us until the war is over—isn't that right, Raymond?"

"Yes," I say. wishing she'd taken me in four and half years ago. "I'm going to stay here until the war is over."

From the first day I arrived on Penry Place until now, more than seventy years later, the strong bond I formed with the Williams family is still with me.

Mr. and Mrs. Williams had two sons and a daughter. Des is the oldest at fifteen, then Gwynneth, I think thirteen, and eleven year old Ieuan. Mr. Williams works in the north dock power station, which incidentally is by a very large petrol dump that the Germans have been trying very hard to destroy. But luckily for everyone, up until now, they've been unsuccessful. I never saw very much of Mr. Williams because of the long hours he worked.

Des, Gwynneth, and Ieuan take me everywhere with them. They treat me just like their little brother. They ask me what games I like. I tell them I like football, running races, and cricket. Des even paints wickets on the garden wall for me. In the summer they take me to Stradey Woods to pick blackberries, and in the winter we collect conkers. Their mother made the deepest impression on me by allowing me to get close to her, which enabled me to throw off all kinds of baggage from my early child-hood. I can't say enough about the kindness and the influence the Williams family had on my life.

When a paper airplane Des had made for me landed on the roof next door, he didn't hesitate to borrow a ladder and climb up for it. A neighbor warned him of the danger of going on the roof just for a paper airplane, but Des told her, "Its Raymond's airplane, I don't mind."

I have a lot of wonderful memories of those days, such as playing on the beach at Pewll Sands with all the family and fishing for goldfish on Pont Twyn with Des and Ieuan. There was the odd Sunday when Des, Gwynneth, and Ieuan would even risk getting themselves in trouble by giving into my suggestion of going to Park Howard instead of chapel.

Mrs. Williams treated me no different than she did her own children. For instance, whenever she knitted a jumper for Ieuan, who was about the same size as me, she'd knit me one as well. Whenever she bought him a new pair of shoes, she'd come back with a pair for me also. Ieuan told me that his toy soldiers and dinky cars that I liked playing with were as much mine as his.

While I write, it brings a lump to my throat to talk about Gwynneth; she passed away a short while ago at the age of seventy. Gwynneth was a young, beautiful looking girl that mothered me just like her mother did. I remember how she'd spend hours helping me with my homework. She even had the patience to play cricket and football with me. I loved her like I did my own sisters.

Although there was an air raid shelter in the garden, we spent most of the time during air raids crouched together in the tight little room under the stairs. Mrs. Williams said she not only felt safer under the stairs, but the air raid shelter was far too cold and damp to sit in all night. She'd sit in between Ieuan and me with her arms wrapped tightly round us both. And when we would fall asleep, as we often did during the very long raids, she wouldn't move a muscle, in case she woke us up. I felt safe in her arms even though I could hear the bombs dropping. In the morning we wouldn't have to go to school until ten o'clock, which we all thought that was great.

There were a few evacuees living around Penry Place, not just me. Anita Bootin, her mother, and her two sisters lived with a lady on Temple Street. And according to my eldest sister Elsie, Ken Dodd, a famous Liverpool comedian, also lived around there.

Everybody's favourite place to play was the "Bankin," which was at the back of the houses. I myself spent hours there, quite often on my own. The times when I was on my own on the "Bankin," Mrs. Williams' instructions to Des, Gwynneth, and Ieuan was that they would have to go round and check every fifteen minutes to see if "our Raymond" was alright. If her children weren't around at the time, she'd stop everything she was doing and go round to have a peep herself. Des came home from school one day to find she was crying. When he asked her what was wrong, she said, "There's nothing wrong really Des, these tears you see are tears of joy. It's just that Raymond has asked me if he could have a house job, like you, Gwynneth, and Ieuan." (The reason for asking for a job was that I desperately wanted to become part of the family, and by her giving me a job like the others, I felt it would give me the right to call her Mammy instead of Auntie.) I'd noticed, for instance, that one of Des' jobs was to make sure the fire bucket was filled with coal, and Ieuan was bring in the sticks to light the fire. So I asked her if I could, in the future, have the job of tying the newspaper in knots instead of her doing it. Let me explain what I mean by that. In order for the paper to burn more slowly, and thus giving the actual firewood more time to catch light, you would take two pages of a newspaper, fold them together forming a tight tube, and then tie a knot in the middle. She was so overjoyed by that simple little request that it made her cry.

Later that year I was moved from St. Peter's School to Copper Works School. I made a lot of new friends in that school. Some were evacuees from different parts of Britain, and some were local Welsh kids. One of the evacuees was a girl by the name of Peggy Duncan, my first serious crush. It wasn't long after arriving there that it became common knowledge that I had a soft spot for Peggy. And it all started off when one of the girls saw me talking to her one day in the vestry doorway behind the church. Most of the other girls didn't like Peggy very much. One of the reasons, I think, was because they were jealous of how pretty she was. And the other reason was they said she had a habit of stealing their boyfriends from them. What I found to be very embarrassing about the whole thing was that some of the girls in our class started to scribble little notes about Peggy and me and then pass them around the class for everyone to read. The one that embarrassed me most of all was the one that'd been written in such a way that it gave the impression that Peggy and I were doing something extremely naughty in the vestry doorway. "We know all about you and Peggy Deacon behind the church. We saw what you were doing. Ha Ha Ha."

This particular note, unfortunately, happened to be the one my teacher found hidden under the books in my desk, and I didn't even know it was there. You can imagine what was going through her mind when she read it. She never said anything, but I could tell by the expression on her face what she was thinking. She ripped the note up, threw it into the wastepaper basket, went over and sat behind her desk, and glared at me for the next ten minutes. Made my face glow bright red. And all Peggy and I did that day in the vestry doorway was no more than talk to each other, that's all, just talk. I know we were there for a long time, but nothing happened.

Every chance they had, either in the schoolyard at playtime, or on my way home, the girls would dance round me and shout, "Raymond Evans has got a girlfriend, Raymond Evans has got a girlfriend." I blushed and tried to convince them otherwise by repeatedly saying, "I haven't … honestly, you ask Peggy." One day in the schoolyard I lost my temper and told them all to piss off. The teacher who overheard my bad language took me into the kitchen and, with a block of soap in her hand, threatened to wash my mouth out. Luckily she decided to keep me back after school instead, and gave me a hundred lines—"I must not say naughty words."

I must admit, I did want to kiss Peggy that day in the vestry doorway, but I was too scared to ask permission. In fact, every time I laid eyes on her, whether it was in the playground or sitting behind her desk, I had this insatiable desire to kiss that beautiful, raven-haired beauty. But having said that, I did find out later that she wouldn't have let me anyway, no matter how much I would have tried to persuade her. "I've no intentions of ever kissing a boy," she told me. "Not until I'm married, that is."

* * * * *

It's the early part of 1943 and the "American invasion" of Llanelli has taken place. No matter where you look, there are "Yanks" everywhere. They drove in the other day, bumper to bumper, hundreds and hundreds of them.

The ladies have gone crazy over these men. They've found it hard to resist the charm of these smart looking soldiers from the "land of movies." In the dance halls, the local men have to look on while the Yanks dance the night away with their girlfriends. These American soldiers are paid so well that they can afford to take the ladies to the pictures not just once, but three times a week if they want to.

And it isn't just the picture houses that the Americans are frequenting so often; the few cafés that are in Llanelli are doing a roaring trade as well. They're not used to eating out so often, these ladies, especially in cafés. Some of them I might tell you, have never even seen the inside of a café before. In fact, before the Yanks came here, they thought they were doing extremely well when their Welsh boyfriends treated them to a bag of fish and chips.

And the kids are just as happy the Yanks have come to town as well. If you ask any evacuee today, I'm sure they'd have no trouble remembering that famous cry, "Got any gum, chum?" I love the sticks of chewing gum they give us; it's much nicer than our chewing gum. And although it's impossible for these Yanks to walk anywhere without some kid pestering them for gum, it doesn't seem to bother them one iota. These soldiers are kind, generous people to a fault. They just smile, stick their hand in their pocket, and say, "Sure kid, there you go."

Jimmy Fielding, one of the Welsh boys in our class, has a sister who is going steady with one of the Yankee soldiers. He tells me she's always coming home with a pair of nylons and a couple of packets of Lucky Strikes in her handbag. He says since his sister has been going out with one of the Yanks, he's stopped smoking Woodbines and changed to Lucky Strikes. He says he likes them much better.

"How long have you been smoking?" I ask him.

"About a year."

"A year? You've been smoking that long?"

"Yeah," he says with a gloating look on his face. "Look, I'm even starting to get nicotine on me fingers."

"How come she gives you cigarettes?"

"She doesn't. I nick them from her handbag." "How many do you nick?"

"One a day until I tasted the Lucky Strike cigarettes, now I've been nicking two a day because I like them so much. They're better than those Woodies my dad smokes, these don't make me cough as much."

"My dad smokes Woodies and they don't make him cough."

"Well they do my dad, he coughs all day long. Me Mam's fed up with his coughing. She's always telling him every ciggy he smokes is another nail in his coffin."

"How about nicking one of those American ciggies for me then?"

"I will if you want me to, but you don't smoke do you?"

"No, but I wouldn't mind trying."

"OK. I'll nick one for you and bring it in tomorrow."

It's playtime the next day and Jimmy and I have just locked ourselves in one of the toilets.

"Did you bring me one?"

"Yeah, but they're not Lucky Strike, they're Camel cigarettes."

"Camel cigarettes? Thought you were bringing Lucky Strike?"

"I was, but when I saw these on her dressing table, I thought I'd try them instead."

"What are they like?"
"Don't know, but I know my sister doesn't like them."

"Why?"

"I heard her telling me Mam when she lit one up. She said to me Mam that they taste so bad, they could even be made out of horse shit."

He strikes the match on the wall and puts the flame to my cigarette. I puff in but the cigarette doesn't light because I keep blowing the match out.

"Suck in, suck in," he says, getting agitated. "You have to suck in to get it lit." After a couple more tries I finally get my cigarette to light. But because I blow the smoke straight out instead of inhaling it, he gets all agitated again.

"Don't just blow the smoke straight out. You're supposed to inhale it first, then blow it out."

"Inhale it?"

"Yes, inhale like this … watch me."

Jimmy lights up and inhales. "Cor, she's right about these," he says, coughing and spluttering. "I think they are made of horse shit."

"It's not that bad," I say, preparing to take another drag.

"Not bad? How do you know if they're not bad? You haven't inhaled yet. Wait until you take a proper drag like I did, then you'll see what I mean."

I put the cigarette between my lips.

"Now take a proper drag this time," Jimmy says. "And don't blow it out, suck it in."

I suck so hard that the insides of my cheeks nearly touch each other.

"That's it," Jimmy shouts. "Now quick, take the cigarette away and breathe in."

I breathe in just like he tells me to ... I wish I hadn't. The moment the smoke hits my lungs, a violent bout of coughing takes over. I'm coughing so loud that Jimmy starts panicking in case one of the teachers hears me. And when the coughing eventually eases off, I become so dizzy that Jimmy has to put his arms around me to hold me up.

"Are you alright Ray?" he asks, holding me against the wall. "You look terrible. You've gone all white."

"Everything's going round and around. I think I'm going to be sick."

"You'll be alright in a minute; it happens to everyone with their first ciggie."

After throwing the cigarette down the toilet, I sit down on the lavatory seat and tell Jimmy that I'll never smoke another ciggie as long as I live, not even a Lucky Strike.

* * * * *

Everyone loves the Americans, not just the kids and young ladies, and it's easy to tell that the Americans love the British people as well. In fact, after the war, a lot of the women left Britain for America to become GI brides. I find it very strange as to why they chose to call the woman GI brides, especially when I found out that GI stands for "government issue."

Chapter 26

Six Years, Six Billets &

A Handful Of Toy Soldiers

It's a cold spring morning in the latter part of April 1945, just a couple of weeks before the Germans formally surrender. Mrs. Williams comes into the bedroom. She creeps passed Ieaun's bed over to mine, places her hand lightly on my shoulder, and whispers in my ear, "Come on Raymond, there's a good boy. It's time to get up now."

For a fleeting moment after I open my eyes, I think it's just another normal day for going to school, and wonder why she's woken me so early—it's still quite dark outside. Then I remember, today I'm not going to school. Today I have to go to the station, and I have to be there early so as to catch the first train back to Liverpool.

"No, Auntie," I say. "Please, I don't want to go back. Let me stay with you."

Mrs. Williams kneels at the side of my bed and holds my

hand. "I'm sorry Raymond," she says. "I told you last night, I'd love for you to stay with me, but it's not possible. Your mother will want you back with her."

"Ask her, when we get to the station, please Auntie, ask her if she'll let you adopt me. Two of my friends in school are getting adopted."

"But surely you'll miss her if you stay here? I know she'll miss you."

"Yes, I'll miss her, but when I leave school and get a job, I'll be able to go on the train and visit her."

She stands up and wipes her eyes. "We'll see," she says. "We'll see when we get to the station."

After five and a half years away, with three of those spent being dumped, often unwanted, in other people's homes, suffering bad bouts of homesickness and depression, finding it difficult to trust anyone, praying for the day the war would come to an end so I could get back to my family, I should have been more than happy to be leaving. But now that the time had actually come to leave, and as much as I loved my Mam and Dad and brothers and sisters, I didn't want to go. I didn't want to be separated from this lady. I'd become far too attached to her. For the past two and a half years she'd showered me with the love and affection that had been missing in my young life since leaving my mother. She'd brought stability back into my life. She'd held me close to her body during those frightening nights under the stairs when the Germans were dropping their bombs. She'd treated me like her own son, not like an evacuee.

While I'm having my breakfast with Des, Gwynneth, and Ieuan, Mrs. Williams is busy packing my things in the little suitcase she bought me yesterday. The only thing I don't need to take with me today is my gas mask. I'm glad I don't need one of those anymore. There's hardly a word spoken around the table between Des, Gwynneth, and me. Then Ieuan comes in and breaks the silence. He has in his hand some toy soldiers his mother had bought him and me when I first arrived there. He says I can give them to one of my little brothers to play with when I get back.

After a very emotional parting from Des, Gwynneth, and Ieuan, Mrs. Williams and I leave for the station. Even some of the neighbors come out to wave goodbye. Mam and everyone else are already at the station when we get there, except Dad and Georgie, of course. Dad is still in Aden, where he's been for that past three years or so, and George, who got his calling up papers a year ago, is in Germany. Mam received a letter from him a few days ago saying he was in some frontline hospital suffering from "Trench Feet" which he apparently got from spending three days trapped down a tank trench.

Mam is sitting on one of the platform seats having a rest when we get to the station. She's tired after carrying the luggage all the way from her billet. When Mrs. Williams sees her, she asks me to go and stand with my brothers and sisters while she has a talk with Mam. She tells Mam how I'm feeling as regards leaving, and says I could stay with her a little longer if Mam agrees.

Mam, seeing how upset Mrs. Williams is, finds it hard to tell her that she can't do that. She thanks her for taking me in and also for the way she's looked after me over the past two and half years, but she has to tell her that she doesn't want to be separated from me or any of her children anymore. Mrs. Williams, trying hard to hold the tears back, tells Mam that she understands perfectly.

When the time comes to board the train, Mrs. Williams puts her arms around me, holds me very tight, and whispers in my ear, "Will you come back to see me one day?"

"Yes, Auntie," I say. "I will."

"Promise?"

"I promise."

As the train moves slowly out of the station, I stand at the window and wave to Mrs. Williams. I can still picture her now, even after all these years. She's the only one left in the empty station, a lonely little figure sitting on the platform seat, holding a hanky to her eyes with one hand and waving with the other. And as the train moves further and further away and begins to round the bend, I have to press my face hard against the glass so I can still see her. And even though she can't see me, she's still sitting on the seat where I'd left her. Waving, just like Mam did in Lime Street six years ago.

Epilogue

July 1966. Devon, England. Going back.

It's Saturday morning, the last day of our holiday here in Devon. Our two children, Raymond and Debbie, are helping me pack the last few things in the car. My wife Lilian is sat on the side of the bed with the road map spread out in front of her, double checking our route back home.

"Come over here for a second," Lilian says. "I want you to see something."

She points to one of the little towns in South Wales that she's drawn a circle around. I bend down to get a closer look.

"It's Llanelli," I say. "The place I was evacuated to."

"Yes," she says. "I just spotted it a few minutes ago when you were downstairs packing the things in the car."

"I don't understand why you are showing me now?"

"Well," she says. "I've been thinking. If you like, we could take a detour on the way home and go to see Mrs. Williams."

I stare at her in shocked silence, not sure whether I've heard her properly. "Mrs. Williams? The lady I was evacuated with?"

"Yes," she says. "We've been talking about going to see her for years, as you know, and now's our chance."

"Yes, I know we have," I say. "And I'd love to see her again, but are we close enough to have the time to go there? I have to go back to work on Monday."

"If we leave right away, we should be there by early evening, giving us enough time to find somewhere to stay for the night. Then on Sunday, before we head back to Whiston, we can spend some time with Mrs. Williams."

* * * * *

It was about seven-thirty in the evening when we finally arrived in Lanelli, and although it had been twenty-one years since I was last there, I didn't have that much of a problem finding my way around.

We stayed at a bed and breakfast that happened to be owned by a man that was one of the volunteers that night in 1939 and had the job of chauffeuring the evacuees from the Evacuee Distribution Centre to their new billets. He and I had a very interesting chat together, which went on until the early hours of the morning.

* * * * *

It's about twelve- thirty the next day, and we're on our way to Penry Place. I wanted to go sooner, straight after our breakfast, but I figured Mrs. Williams would probably be at church. So, for the past couple of hours I've been driving around showing my wife and children the different billets where I stayed.

The one Lilian was most interested in seeing was Mrs. Simmons'. Whether Mrs. Simmons was still living there, I wasn't sure, but even if she was, I didn't want to find out. The children couldn't understand why I refused to knock on her door and tell her who I was, but it would have brought back too many painful memories.

Penry Place looked even smaller than I remembered it to be. I sat for a few moments, looking around and collecting my thoughts.

My eyes kept going to the little house in the top left-hand corner, Mrs. Williams', number six. The front door used to be brown; now it was a bright shiny red. "I wonder if she still lives there," I said to Lilian. "She may have moved on to somewhere else."

"Well, the only way you're going to find out," she said, "is to go and knock."

I got out of the car, crossed over the street, and walked slowly up to the house. My stomach began to do a dance as I got nearer to her front door. *What am I going to say to her? Will she still want to see me after all this time? Is she still alive?*

After pressing the doorbell several times and getting no answer, I started back toward the car wondering whether she had moved to live somewhere else, disappointed not to have been able to see her again.

"I've got a feeling she doesn't live there anymore," I said to Lilian, getting back into the car. "Twenty-one years is a long time; she could be living anywhere."

"She may not have come back from church. Let's go and get something to eat and call back later."

Just as I'm about to start the engine up, I hear someone shouting. I look up and see a little grey-haired lady standing on Mrs. Williams' step, frantically waving.

"Hello," she shouts. "Can I help you?"

I step out of the car and shield the sun from my eyes to get a better look.

"It's her," I tell Lilian. "It's Mrs. Williams. I'm sure it is."

"Well, don't keep her waiting," she says. "Quick, go and tell her who you are."

It was her all right—I would have recognized her anywhere, even though her dark brown hair had turned grey and there were wrinkles on her face.

"I'm sorry," she said, in her wonderful, lilting Welsh accent. "I was in the garden."

"You won't remember me, Mrs. Williams," I said. "It was a long time ago, but you took me in as an evacuee during … "

Her eyes filled with tears. "Raymond?" she said, not giving me a chance to finish. "Is it really you?"

I couldn't speak; all I could do to answer was to give her a nod. She came out onto the pavement, flung her arms around me, and whispered in my ear, "You came back to see me—I always knew you would."

It was intensely emotional, meeting that lady again, and then later Des and Ieuan and Gwynneth.

✶ ✶ ✶ ✶ ✶

That afternoon, when we were all gathered around the table enjoying Mrs. Williams' famous Welsh scones and Bara Bryth and talking about old times, I took the opportunity to thank her for taking me in and treating me as if I was her "other" son.

She was a beautiful person through and through. I stayed with her for the last two and a half years of the war, but those two and a half years were enough for that lady to mold me into what I am today.

Just before we left that afternoon, she took my hand and led me upstairs into the little bedroom that Ieuan and I once shared. She opened the drawer of the bedside cabinet. Inside was an assortment of toy soldiers, the very same toy soldiers she had bought me the day after she took me in. "Every time I've opened this drawer and looked at those little toy soldiers," she said, "they've reminded me of you. You spent many, many hours sitting in front of the fire playing with them. You left them on the table. Do you remember? It was the morning you were leaving to go back to Liverpool."

"Yes," I said. "I remembered them when the train was pulling out of the station."

"Well, here you are," she said, handing them to me. "You can take them now. I knew you would come back one day, so I've kept them for you. Not to play with, of course, I know you're too old for that … just as a little keepsake."

Six months later Ieuan wrote to me to tell me his mother had passed away. He thanked me for going back to see her before she died, and said that he hoped Lilian and I would still keep in touch with them. His letter also said that after we left that day, his mother had told them that she'd always cherished two wishes in her life, one was to see the Queen in person, and the other was to see me again. "I know I haven't seen the Queen as of yet," she told them. "And I know now that I probably never will, but I don't care anymore, not now that I've seen Raymond."

Before The Last All Clear
voted

#1 Readers Choice

2008 Welsh Books Council Year of Reading
(English Language Selection)

Other books by Ray Evans

Synopsis

During World War II over three million mothers and their children were evacuated under the British Government's "Operation Pied Piper."

Ray Evans, age 6 at the time, was one of those children. Separated from his family and home he wasn't able to return to Liverpool until he was 12

Experiences like Ray's, inevitably change and affect us, especially the very young. Many of those experiences, the horrible, sometimes hilarious and eventually happy, were shared in his previous memoir Before The Last All Clear.

All I Want is a Peaceful World...and a Pork Pie! Picks up Ray's story as he returns to Liverpool, to be reunited with his parents and siblings.

Join Ray on his amazing life journey, as he struggles to make sense of the desolation he finds in war ravaged Liverpool, his years as a young adult doing his National Service in Egypt, his romance with Lilian, now his bride of 57 years, and the entrepreneurial spirit that propelled him to start his own successful business.

See how Ray's evacuation experiences shaped his character, influenced his mindset, brought his innate sense of determination to the fore and helped him define his own future. They say hindsight is 20:20 but Ray has always chosen to focus on the future because, as he explains "That's where we are the architects of our own lives!"

Live the roller coaster of joy, disappointment and frustration

- As Ray returns home to Liverpool.
- As he finds himself, in a war zone again!
- As he strives to make a life better than he was born into.
- As he starts over, and over again.
- Always reaching for the light at the end of the tunnel
  - his dream of "being his own boss!"

Watch video trailers and learn more about our VIP Reader programs for schools, colleges, reading groups, book clubs, fund raising and charity events at:

BeforeTheLastAllClear.com

RayEvansAuthor.com

VIP Reader Programs

Meet 'n Greet, Fund Raisers & Book Signings:

Ray is available to meet with book clubs, reading groups, schools and academic institutions in person based on location or via Skype and video conferencing through his VIP Reader Programs.

Book signings and fund raising events typically incorporate our exclusive narrated video covering a brief background explanation about Britain during WWII and Operation Pied Piper. This is typically followed by a Q&A discussion of how Ray's early life experiences shaped him and his life as an adult.

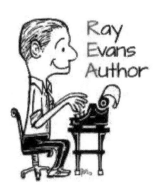

Contact us for more information or to schedule an event:

RayEvansAuthor.com/Contact

Connect With Ray:

Follow Ray on Twitter:

@RayEvansAuthor

Facebook:

Facebook.com/RayEvansAuthor

Author Blog:

RayEvansAuthor.com

Author Bio

Born in Liverpool, England in 1933 into a family of 7, Ray Evans was evacuated to the South Wales town of Llanelli at the outbreak of World War Two. He remained there until the cessation of hostilities in 1945, when he and his family were returned to Liverpool to re-build their family and their lives.

Despite his initial dislike of being in South Wales and Llanelli, he grew to love the beautiful Welsh countryside and learned firsthand of the love and genuine warmth of the Welsh people. Now feeling like a duck out of water yet again, but yearning for the gently rolling hills and green valleys of South Wales, Ray vowed he would move out of the city as soon as he possibly could.

When he left school Ray worked first at the State Restaurant in Liverpool as a cooks apprentice and then for Hanson's Dairy as a delivery man before going into the Army to complete his two years National Service as a member of the Royal Army Medical Corps in Egypt.

He returned to Liverpool and in 1956 married his wife Lilian and shortly thereafter moved out of the city limits to the small village of Whiston. Lilian and Ray have one son and a daughter. In 1964 Ray started a wholesale clothing business and he and Lilian ran this enterprise together highly successfully until 1995, when they moved to the USA to be closer to their daughter and grandaughter (the inspiration for his writing the book).

Shortly after moving there Ray began writing the book at the suggestion of his daughter and with the encouragement of Lilian to help ensure the stories would be passed on to all of their grandchildren and generations to come.

In 2001 the family moved once more and settled in the gentle rolling hills and green fields near Williamsburg, Virginia, which with all its history and connections to England feels just like home. The first edition of Before the Last All Clear was published in 2005, with a second edition released to the American market in August 2008, being published on Kindle in 2011.

The most common question Ray was asked at book signings and events was, "what happened after the war?" That's what inspired him to write the next part of his memoir "All I Want Is A Peaceful World…& A Pork Pie!"

In the process of writing the books, Ray came to realise more than ever before, how the importance of having a home had impacted his life during the evacuation and far beyond. He supports many related charities by actively participating in fund raising events.

Glossary:

This is a very brief alphabetical list of non-technical explanations for some of the slang terms and typically British names for things that are referred to throughout the book.

Bin = Garbage can or garbage bin.

Clothing Coupons = When you went to buy clothes you not only needed the money but also to have the ration coupons to allow you to buy.

Cobblers = Shoe maker and repair shop.

Cranking the engine = The original method to start an engine was to use a metal 'crank' to turn the engine over in order to get it running.

Dinner Time = Typically a meal eaten around 6-8 PM.

Doolally = Slag for silly or crazy.

Fortnight = Fourteen days.

Gerry = Derogatory slang term for Germans commonly used to refer to the enemy troops either singular or plural.

Get Your Skates On – Hurry up.

Handbag = Refers to what is commonly called a pocket-book or purse in the US. (see purse).

Haversack = Bag with a shoulder strap for ease of carrying. They were often made from waste or left over sacking material as many people could not afford suit cases to put their children's belongings into.

Jersey or Jumper = Sweater.

Pantomime or Panto = Stage production, aimed at families and children. Often with musical numbers and loosely based on a fairy tale or children's story with slapstick comedic elements where the audience is encouraged to participate, sing along and shout out to performers.

The Pictures = Slang term for cinema or movie theatre.

Plasticine = A common brand of modelling clay similar to Play-Doh.

Plimsolls = Canvas shoes, cheap and readily available, although not particularly good in cold or wet weather.

Po = Slang term for the chamber pot or potty, still in fairly common use in many homes during the war as only affluent homes would have had indoor plumbing.

Purse = In the UK a purse is what a woman keeps her money in, typically with compartments for both paper notes and coin. It is not a bag as in the US (see handbag).

Ration Books = Many things were rationed during WWII and for a number of years afterwards. Food, Clothing, Gasoline among them.

Registry Office = **Local** government office where the registry of births, deaths and marriages would be recorded.

Satchel = Soft sided bag with a shoulder strap that allows for it to be carried hanging across the body diagonally. Often used for carrying school books.

Scabies = Highly contagious parasite that causes severe itching and leaves a rash. Caused by an infestation with a parasite that burrows under the skin. It was commonly passed along during the war when more than one child would be sharing a bed. It is typically spread by close skin to skin contact often through holding hands.

Shilling, Sixpence and Pennies = Units of money, coins

Tea Time = Typically a lighter meal eaten around 4-6 PM although in northern England and especially among the working class this is really the main meal of the day and takes the place of dinner.

Ten Bob Note = Paper money – Value ten shillings.

Thruppence = Three penny piece, often called a "thru'penny bit" had 12 sides (dodecagonal).

Vicar = Similar to a priest or minister, in some Church of England parishes there may be a Rector rather than a vicar.

Welsh = The national language of Wales.

Wireless = Battery powered radio.

* * * * *

British Monetary System

One last thing that probably requires explanation especially for anyone who didn't grow up in the UK before the "other D-Day". British money today is based on a decimal system where 100 pennies equals one pound, it's a very simple and straight forward system, that was actually only introduced on 15th February 1971.

Prior to that the British (pre-decimalisation) system of coinage was introduced by King Henry II (Henry was a Plantagenet – essentially meaning he was 'mostly' French even though he was King of England at the time) around 1158, although he continued to 'tweak' the system and the coins, through about 1180.

Anyway what's important to know, is that the system was based on the troy weight of precious metals. So the 'penny' was literally one 'pennyweight' of silver. A pound sterling weighed in at 240 pennyweights, or a 'pound of sterling silver'.

The symbols 's' for shilling and 'd' for pence were derived from the Latin solidus and denarius used in the Middle Ages. The '£' sign developed from the 'l' for libra.

£ or l in some documents = pound

s or /- = shilling (from the solidus, a Roman coin)

d = penny (from the 'denarius', a Roman coin)

g or gn = guinea

The half-crown was a denomination of British money worth half of a crown, and was the equivalent of two and a half shillings, or one-eighth of a pound. The half-crown coin was first issued in 1549, in the reign of Edward VI.

There were twenty (20) shillings to a pound.

There were twelve (12) pennies to a shilling.

A penny could be sub-divided into two half pennies or four farthings (quarter pennies – which were legal tender right up until 31st December 1960).

> 2 farthings = 1 halfpenny (ha'penny)
>
> 2 halfpennies = 1 penny (1d)
>
> 3 pence = 1 thruppence (3d) (a thru'penny bit)
>
> 6 pence = 1 sixpence (a 'tanner') (6d)
>
> 12 pence = 1 shilling (a bob) (1s)
>
> 2 shillings = 1 florin (a 'two bob bit') (2s)
>
> 2 shillings and 6 pence = 1 half-crown (2s 6d)
>
> 5 shillings = 1 Crown (5s)

The old £1 coin (as opposed to today's £1 coin which is gold in colour) was called a Sovereign and was actually made of gold.

A paper one pound note was and still is often referred to as a 'quid'. There are also five £5, ten £10, twenty £20 and fifty £50 pound notes. In Scotland and Ireland you may even see £100 notes in circulation.

> 1 guinea = £1-1s-0d (£1/1/-) = one pound and one shilling = 21 shillings
>
> (which is £1.05 in today's money)
>
> 1 guinea might be shown on a sign or written as '1g' or '1gn'.

A guinea was considered a more gentlemanly amount than £1. You paid tradesmen, like say a carpenter, in pounds but gentlemen, such as an artist, would typically be paid in guineas.

> A third of a guinea was equal to exactly seven shillings.

Why was it called a guinea? Because the Guinea coast was fabled for its gold, so its name became attached to other things with similarly perceived high value, including but not limited to, the protectorate of British New Guinea in 1884.

NOTES:

27378447R00157

Made in the USA
Columbia, SC
23 September 2018